"For those who think the high rate of divorce is simply a product of the times and there's not much we can do about it, this slim volume provides a great deal of hope. There <u>are</u> answers, and Michael McManus in *Insuring Marriage: 25 Proven Ways to Prevent Divorce* presents them in the form of fresh stories of actual experiences. This book should be read by those considering marriage, those thinking about ending their marriages, and even those who want their marriage to remain happy and intact."

George H. Gallup, Jr.
Gallup International Institute

"The church can no longer turn its back on the problem of divorce. I am encouraged to see, at last, resources that meet this problem head on with valuable, workable solutions that are already making a difference. It is now possible, with these tested and effective methods, to stop the relentless tide of divorce once and for all. Mike McManus' *Marriage Savers* resources need to find their way into every church around the world."

Dr. Jimmy Draper, President
Baptist Sunday School Board

"Too many people get divorced far too easily. Michael McManus gives solid practical advice on how to avoid divorce. It is the kind of advice that is biblically sound but devoid of worn out pieties. This is good stuff."

Tony Campolo, Writer/Speaker

"I am delighted to do all that I can to encourage 'Marriage Savers' and think this absolutely must be a very, very high priority."

The Most Rev. William H. Keeler
President, National Conference
of Catholic Bishops

Insuring Marriage

25 PROVEN WAYS
TO PREVENT DIVORCE

MICHAEL J. MCMANUS

ZondervanPublishingHouse
Grand Rapids, Michigan

A Division of HarperCollins*Publishers*

Insuring Marriage
© Copyright 1994 • Michael J. McManus

Requests for information should be addressed to:
📕 Zondervan Publishing House
Grand Rapids, Michigan 49530

Library of Congress Cataloging-in-Publication Data
McManus, Michael J.
    Insuring marriage : 25 proven ways to prevent
divorce / Michael J. McManus.
        p.   cm.
    Originally published: Nashville, Tenn. : Lifeway,
c1994.
    ISBN: 0-310-20740-1 (softcover)
    1. Marriage—Religious aspects—Christianity.
I. Title.
[BV835.M345   1996]
248.4—dc20   95-43825
                                                    CIP

Printed in the United States of America

96 97 98 99 /LP/ 10 9 8 7 6 5 4

Dedicated

to couples whose marriages have been joyous,
growing experiences for decades, who have a
heart to serve as mentors to the seriously dating,
engaged, or newlyweds, or perhaps to those in
deeply troubled marriages and to pastors
who will "prepare God's people for works
of service," as marriage savers.

ACKNOWLEDGMENTS

I would never have written this book if it were not for Harriet, my wife and best friend for nearly three decades. She has added so much joy to my life, and our marriage grew so profoundly through our Marriage Encounter weekend that I developed an interest in other ways to save or strengthen marriages. She has also been the more active partner of our work as a mentor couple in working with seriously dating and engaged couples and in training other mentors.

I'm grateful to the 100+ newspapers which first published many of these "answers" on how to avoid divorce in my nationally syndicated column, "Ethics and Religion." I also want to thank Zondervan for publishing my first book, *Marriage Savers,* which has sparked a movement within denominations and communities to do a better job preparing couples for marriage and sustaining existing ones.

One of the first people to read *Marriage Savers* and see its potential was Dr. Jimmy Draper, President of the Baptist Sunday School Board. He was the first national religious leader to recognize the many practical ways that churches could become "marriage savers." He also saw the importance of producing materials that could help other denominations preserve marriages.

I also want to express my appreciation to Joe Musser, the producer of six "Marriage Saver Videos" that make these answers come alive, who in his spare time, also contributed to this book.

Finally, I want to thank **you** for buying this book. My prayer is that it will help you build a lifelong marriage.

Michael J. McManus
October 1994

FOREWORD

Christians are reading the news these days and rubbing their eyes in amazement. Suddenly the world seems to be waking up to the crucial role morality plays in public policy.

First the sophisticated *Atlantic Monthly* magazine startled readers with an article announcing "Dan Quayle Was Right" showing the harm that children suffer from family breakdown. Then the *Wall Street Journal* published an article by social scientist Charles Murray, arguing that illegitimacy is the most reliable predictor of a host of social pathologies— poverty, crime, drug abuse, and welfare dependency.

All our vaunted poverty, welfare, and drug programs have less effect, it turns out, than decisions made by individual men and women to wait for marriage and maturity before they have children. Our most pressing social problems stem from moral decisions made in the heart of family life.

This realization could mean a dramatic new openness to Christian ethics. For decades public policy was pursued as though it could ignore moral questions. But now policy makers recognize that when a society's moral sense decays—particularly in regard to the family—the center cannot hold.

For the church, this represents a remarkable opportunity. By equipping Christians for strong marriages, we can set an example, demonstrating that there are answers to society's most pressing social crisis. To be salt in a decaying society, the church must boldly preach the biblical ethics of sex and marriage. We must take a strong stance against premarital sex and cohabitation. With *Insuring Marriage: 25 Proven Ways to Prevent Divorce,* Michael McManus gives us just the tools we need for the task.

First, this book gives statistics to back up biblical teachings. For example, one study found that those who engage in premarital sexual relations are 71 percent more likely to divorce than those who remain virgins. McManus also provides statistics that identify the need to adopt biblical teachings. For example, he states that though 75 percent of American weddings are blessed by a pastor, priest, or rabbi, six out of ten new marriages will fail.

Second, churches should make use of the programs listed here to help build strong marriages. For teens, abstinence programs teach how to resist sexual temptation. For engaged couples, a premarital questionnaire can spotlight problem areas and even predict who will divorce. Married couples can attend enrichment retreats. Couples in deeply troubled marriages can participate in programs that restore their relationship.

Third, a church can avoid being a "wedding factory" by setting standards for couples that ask for a church wedding. McManus describes an exciting project called a Community Marriage Policy that has the potential of cutting a community's divorce rate.

Restoring the family is one area where the church should be taking the lead. The government can't. The media isn't. The schools aren't. You and I need to take up the task of equipping people for strong marriages. This book can be our manual for getting started.

Christians have long argued the importance of private morality in shaping public virtue. By becoming marriage savers, we can make that point dramatically—and in the process fight the most virulent cancer eating at the heart of our culture.

Charles Colson
Washington, DC, 1994

Introduction

Getting married in America has become a gamble—a losing gamble. More than half of all new marriages are failing. Are you in such a marriage? Perhaps you or those close to you have considered divorce. Or, if unmarried, are you afraid of making the wrong choice?

If so, *Insuring Marriage: 25 Proven Ways to Prevent Divorce* is for you! The basic thesis of this book is that **divorce can be prevented**. Some of you may be asking yourselves, "Why should I stay in a bad marriage?" Let me quote a respected family author and advocate:

"Don't permit the possibility of divorce to enter your thinking. Even in moments of great conflict and discouragement, divorce is no solution."[1]

James Dobson

Most people assume, wrongly, that it's impossible to improve a bad marriage. Don't despair. There are answers! In fact, even marriages with serious problems can be saved.

This book offers principles for "marriage insurance" to help you prevent divorce by learning how to build a lifelong marriage. The good news is that **there is hope**.

- Bad marriages can be avoided before they begin.
- Engaged couples can be provided "marriage insurance."
- Existing marriages can be strengthened.
- Deeply troubled marriages can be saved.
- Separated couples can rebuild their marriages.
- Divorce rates can be decreased.

What's Wrong With Divorce?

Before offering suggestions on how to avoid divorce, let's consider what is wrong with divorce. Here are four major reasons to avoid divorce.

1. Scripture Speaks Against Divorce

Scripturally, divorce is condemned in both the Old and New Testaments. The Bible's position against divorce is clear. Jesus spoke against divorce (Matt. 19) and the Old Testament writer Malachi predicts three negative consequences of divorce: great sorrow; a distress that prayer can't help; and children of divorce are likely to be rebellious, not "godly offspring" (see Mal. 2:13-16). The biblical message is so hard that some pastors are reluctant to preach on it. This is a grievous disservice to their congregations who come to believe that they can divorce with the Lord's blessing.

2. Divorce Is Harmful to Children

When a child loses a parent to divorce the child is bound to be affected in some way by the loss. Karl Zinsmeister says in an article in *The American Enterprise* that there is vast scientific evidence showing that kids are the casualties when families break up in divorce. They end up with intellectual, physical, and emotional scars. He says that the drug crisis, the crisis in our schools, and the problems of teen pregnancy and juvenile crime can be traced to one predominant source—broken families, the result of divorce.

Most divorces lead to remarriage, but to different spouses. And since 60 percent of remarriages fail, the odds are that a second divorce will occur before their children reach age 18. Thus, half the children of divorce may experience a broken home more than once before they graduate from high school.

3. Poverty Is Often a Result of Divorce

Do responsible parents want their children to live in poverty? In 1991, a National Commission on Children reported that when parents divorce or separate, children are the victims. Youngsters living with one parent, usually their mothers, are six times as likely to be living at the poverty level than kids who live with both parents. Other studies confirm that kids do best when they have the attention and financial support of **both** father and mother in a stable marriage.

Only 15.5 percent of divorced mothers receive alimony—and usually only for a year or two.[2] And what about child support? Only a small fraction of divorced mothers get full child support. And "full" payments for many are not large: *$150 per month*!

4. The Pain of Divorce Continues for Adults

According to the book, *Second Chances* by Judith Wallerstein and Sandra Blakslee, in 90 percent of the cases either the former husband or wife (or both) is still in pain ten years after divorce.[3]

These findings come as a complete surprise to most Americans who believe that divorce is just another crisis to be dealt with so that the parties can "get on with their lives."

However, years after divorce, most families still suffer the anguish. Everyone in the family is wounded, angry, and most still haven't gotten their lives together. The adults of divorce have unexpected emotional and behavioral problems with their children.

A woman whose marriage ended in divorce a decade ago told me, "Divorce is like suffering death without a funeral. The pain never ends."

So, you can readily see that for everyone involved finding ways to improve a marriage is better than dissolving it.

DIVORCE IS USUALLY NO ANSWER

In certain cases couples should separate—where physical abuse, persistent alcoholism, or adultery is present. However, according to a Gallup Poll, only 5 percent of marriages are dissolved due to physical abuse; 16 percent of divorces were attributed to alcoholism; and 17 percent to adultery. The overwhelming cause of divorce is *incompatibility* (47 percent) and *arguments* over money, family or children (10 percent).[4]

In other words, nearly 60 percent of all divorces are caused by poor communication. **These are the very marriages which most easily can be saved.**

BE A MARRIAGE SAVER

The "25 Proven Ways to Prevent Divorce" in this book are treated as answers to the question, **"What can I do?"** They are written succinctly to give a quick overview of steps to prepare for marriage or to strengthen an existing marriage. Most of the "Answers" will only whet your appetite, so each concludes with suggestions on where to learn more. Two are mentioned regularly:

- *Marriage Savers*, a book packed with details on how you, your church, and community can be a marriage saver.
- *Marriage Savers Resource Collection*, a series of six videos featuring people you will read about in this book. The collection also includes a copy of this book and *Marriage Savers*.

Please don't miss the Marriage Savers Declaration at the end of this book. I hope you will sign it as an expression of your commitment to insuring marriages.

Insuring Marriage: 25 Proven Ways to Prevent Divorce is written to give you hope. My prayer for you is that you may bond with another in marriage to bring joy to your life. Then I hope you will share what you've learned and **be a marriage saver!**

Michael J. McManus

[1] James C. Dobson, *Love for a Lifetime*, (Portland: Multnomah Press, 1987), 103.

[2] National Commission on Children. *Beyond Rhetoric: A New American Agenda for Children and Families*. Final Report. Washington, D.C., 1991.

[3] Judith Wallerstein and Sandra Blakslee, *Second Chances*, (New York: Ticknor & Fields, 1989), XV.

[4] Michael J. McManus, *Marriage Savers*, (Grand Rapids: Zondervan, 1993), 123.

Insuring Marriage

How Can I Become a Marriage Saver?

25 Answers

Basics for Being a Marriage Saver
1. Marriage Is Vulnerable to Divorce: Heed the Warning Signs
2. Take Seriously What the Bible Says About Key Issues Related to Divorce
3. Help Your Church Insure Future Marriages

Helping Single Adults and Seriously Dating Couples
4. Help Teenagers Abstain from Sex
5. Beware of Sexual Entrapments!
6. Don't Live Together in a Trial Marriage
7. Seriously Dating Couples Can Avoid Mistakes
8. Learn From a Relationship That Doesn't Lead to Marriage

Marriage Insurance for Engaged Couples
9. Use a Premarital Inventory to Identify Strengths and Weaknesses
10. Help Insure and Save Marriages by Being a Mentor Couple
11. Participate in a Premarital Retreat to Improve Communication Skills
12. Invest Time and Energy in Marriage Preparation

Helping Couples Strengthen Their Marriage

Even Deeply Troubled Marriages Can Be Saved

Helping the Separated or Divorced and Stepfamilies

Be a Marriage Saver

Marriage Savers Declaration

A N S W E R 1

Insuring Marriage

Heed the Warning Signs of a Troubled Relationship

Relationships between men and women tend to go through phases which are predictable—but always seem surprising to those involved. First, there is the glow of romance in which a beloved can do no wrong. Then comes a time of growing disillusionment when they can do nothing right!

At that point, mature people recognize that they must invest more of themselves to **build a lasting relationship.** Conversely, immature people react poorly. They whine and complain and drive the relationship toward the rocks.

In fact, the natural direction of male-female relationships in America of the 1990s is to **separate**. Centrifugal forces drive people apart. He gets involved in his work and his hobbies, and she gets involved in her work and the children. Disillusionment builds as they drift apart.

But to be forewarned is to be forearmed.

You can build a marriage relationship that will endure if you are selfless rather than selfish and if you make the Lord the third partner in the relationship. That, in a nutshell, is the message of this book. This book is packed with suggestions on how to deal with a wide range of warning signs for dating couples and the already married. The chapters are written as **Answers** for each stage of the marital life cycle beginning with teenagers, then moving to seriously dating couples, a warning to those tempted to enter a "trial marriage," giving engaged couples "marriage insurance," providing a number of ways to strengthen existing marriages and save even the most deeply troubled ones, ideas to reconcile the separated and divorced, and ending with ways to make stepfamilies successful. Answer 1 will summarize warning signs that will be discussed in the following chapters.

WARNING SIGNS OF TROUBLE

Warning signs of trouble reveal themselves at whatever your stage of life may be. Many people have an idealistic view of marriage and are often "blindsided" by the problems that lead to divorce. Newlyweds are often astounded by the conflict that comes early to their marriage. After the wedding, a period of adjustment sets in, and the charm and enchantment of dating and courtship is but a blurred recollection.

FIRST YEAR CHECKUP

If you are married, consider your first year of marriage. Check all areas that apply.

We found ourselves in regular conflict over:

___ money management
___ time with each other
___ expectations
___ his/her family
___ church involvement
___ other: _____

How many areas did you check? If you are in your first year of marriage and checked more than one, discuss these with a counselor or your pastor. These can be warning signs for future conflict.

Warning signs can be a signal that a relationship may be vulnerable to separation and divorce. Many of the warning signs could have been noticed while couples were seriously dating or engaged.

WARNING SIGNS FOR THE DATING COUPLE
• Premature sexual involvement.
Studies show that unmarried couples who have sex before marriage are more likely to divorce. Conversely, virgins have a much better chance of a lifelong marriage relationship. Here is evidence that Paul was right when he encouraged the Corinthians to "flee sexual immorality" (1 Cor. 6:18).

DIVORCE PREVENTION INVENTORY FOR SINGLE ADULTS

____ I am single and currently engaging in sexual intercourse with the opposite sex.

____ I am single and in a dating relationship that has become physically intense too soon.

If you checked either of these, consider making a commitment to abstain from sexual intercourse before marriage. Work on deepening your relationship as friends. Give it time to develop.

The emphasis from our society is on convincing young people that premarital sex is OK. This message is promoted in school, on TV, in motion pictures, magazines, and music. Even in this day of AIDS and high rates of teen pregnancy it is rare to hear a message of sexual abstinence or chastity.

• Too much time together.

Couples who spend too much time together in a relationship, long before an engagement, may fall into the trap of too much intimacy that leads to pre-marital sex.

Dr. Jim Talley suggests couples find ways of cutting back on the time they spend alone with each other in order to protect themselves from being "too close too soon." He suggests you first build a friendship, then a marriage.

• Ignorance about the other person.

Since most people don't reveal the "warts" to the person they are trying to impress, many important aspects of a relationship are ignored until after the wedding.

As these details emerge, so do the problems. Some problems are so serious they can break a marriage apart. Reason dictates, to learn as much as possible about each other *before* the wedding.

Caution signs should go up if a seriously dating couple cannot answer the most basic questions about each other. Questions include: What is his/her family background? What is his/her social, economic, ethnic, religious, and moral background?

Couples have to feel more than just a sexual attraction for their marriage to succeed. When there are extreme differences in their backgrounds, the stage is set for potential marital mayhem.

• A lack of instruction and training.

If we want to drive a car without complications or collisions, we study driver education and take tests to prove that we have learned what we were taught.

Yet, when we come to the serious, lifelong consideration of marriage, little instruction is offered. The church can provide this training for the nearly and newly married. Many suggestions will be made for instruction throughout this book.

WARNING SIGNS FOR THE MARRIED COUPLE

Certain signs in a marriage relationship can alert us to potential conflict and the possibility of divorce. Check the following warning signs that may apply to your relationship. Suggestions for addressing these warning signs will be provided throughout this book in the Answers that follow.

___ *The number and frequency of arguments.*

Disagreements are natural. They don't have to be ugly. There are ways to resolve conflict that are healthy and can actually strengthen a relationship. Married couples must learn how to deal constructively with conflict.

___ *The tendency of one (or both) of the spouses to be overtly critical of the other mate.* Putting down your spouse in public or in other ways destroying his/her love, intimacy, or trust eventually damages the relationship.

___ *The loss of self-confidence and assurance.* When a spouse lacks the self-confidence to demand respect from a mate, one of two things will happen—both negative. Either the weaker person will placate the bully, or the bully will lose so much respect that he or she will find someone else to respect and will push for a divorce. Also, if one of the partners shows poor self-esteem or feels ignored, abandoned, or betrayed by the other partner, serious trouble lies ahead.

___ *Financial areas.* Financial disagreements cause many of the problems in a marriage. Married couples should resolve how money will be spent.

___ *Questions concerning children can be warning signs.* Does each partner share similar ideas of family planning? Will you have children—if so, how many—and when? Will Mom (or Dad) stay home with them while the other spouse works—or will both parents work?

These warning signs cover a variety of potential problem areas that couples need to address before the situation becomes critical. Divorce is generally a decision that is arrived at over a period of time— few divorces are the result of spontaneous blow-ups.

When the warning signs begin to surface, the wise couple will find ways to deal with them in positive, constructive methods. If you checked any of the warning signs listed here, seek help through time together, counseling, a mentor couple, or group study. And continue reading the Answers in this book!

Biblical References

Matthew 7:24, 25; Ephesians 5:25, 28; Colossians 3:18, 19; 1 Peter 3:7

Other Resources

1. *Marriage Savers* by Michael McManus (Zondervan, 1993), chapters 2 and 3.

2. *Restoring a Loving Marriage* by Jay Kesler with Joe Musser (David C. Cook, 1989).

3. *Too Close Too Soon* by Jim Talley and Bobbie Reed. (Thomas Nelson, 1982) Call 1-800-645-3761 to order direct from Jim Talley.

A N S W E R 2

Insuring Marriage

Take Seriously What the Bible Says About Key Issues Related to Divorce

Since sex outside of marriage, cohabitation, and other moral and ethical problems are contributing factors to divorce, we must look to Scripture to find answers. The church can prevent divorce by upholding God's standards. Let's consider three examples, their applications, and the biblical standards.

Key Issue: Broken pledge of faithfulness
Biblical Standard: Faithfulness in marriage
Biblical Reference: Malachi 2:13-16; Matthew 19:9
Malachi's indictment on divorce extended to the people as a whole:

> You flood the Lord's altar with tears. You weep and wail because he no longer pays attention to your offerings or accepts them with pleasure from your hands. You ask, "Why?" It is because the Lord is acting as the witness between you and the wife of your youth, because you have broken faith with her, though she is your partner, the wife of your marriage covenant.

Has not the Lord made them one? In flesh and spirit they are his. And why one? Because he was seeking godly offspring. So guard yourself in your spirit, and do not break faith with the wife of your youth. "I hate divorce," says the Lord God of Israel.

Key Issue: Cohabitation
Biblical Standard: Cease cohabiting until marriage, abstain from premarital sex
Biblical References: John 4:18; 1 Corinthians 6:18; 1 Thessalonians 4:3-5

In 1993 I spoke to pastors from 16 denominations in 10 southern cities and asked them, "How many of you have preached a sermon on cohabitation?"

In city after city, not one hand went up. So I told them: "You are part of the problem. Scripture is certainly clear on this issue. In his letter to the Corinthians Paul says, 'Flee sexual immorality.' So why haven't you preached about the wrongs of cohabitation?"

Perhaps they did not know that there is *sociological evidence* of the harm of unmarried men and women living together *which supports the biblical position.* (Cohabitation and premarital sex will be discussed in detail later in this book.)

Key Issue: The church's failure to address lax moral standards
Biblical Standard: Value-based morality embraced by believers
Biblical References: Malachi 2:8; 1 Corinthians 6:9-10; 1 Thessalonians 4:3-5

The church's failure to teach about divorce is no better now than it was in fifth century B.C. Israel. Malachi 2:8 says, "But you have turned from the way and by your teaching have caused many to stumble."

About three-fourths of all first marriages are blessed by pastors, priests, and rabbis, according to the National Center for Health Statistics. Yet six out of ten new marriages end in divorce or separation.

Thus, the church itself is part of the divorce problem. Clearly, organized religion has had a direct role in establishing most marriages. But in too many cases the church has often acted as a **"blessing machine"** that has no more impact on the couple than a justice of the peace. Too many churches have deteriorated to being little more than a **"wedding factory"** offering a borrowed chapel, a hired pastor, and a rented organist.

IDEAS FOR BEING A MARRIAGE SAVER

Both premarital sexual activity and cohabitation should be denounced by Christians—just as Paul denounced it for the church at Corinth. (See 1 Cor. 6:13, 18-20; 10:13.)

Teachers, utilize the opportunities you have to teach others in small-group settings.

Pastors, preach on these issues, taking advantage of annual family emphases and sermon series.

Counselors, advise couples of the dangers and point them to the biblical truths.

Couples and *individuals,* encourage others you know to become acquainted with these truths and facts by sharing with them a copy of this book and God's Word.

Biblical References
Malachi 2:8, 13-16; 1 Corinthians 6:13, 18-20; 10:13; 1 Thessalonians 4:3; Hebrews 13:4

Other Resources
1. *Marriage Savers* by Michael McManus (Zondervan, 1993), chapters 2 and 3.
2. Have your pastor view *Marriage Savers Resource Collection,* especially video programs 1, 2, and 3.

A N S W E R   3

Insuring *Marriage*

Help Your Church Insure Future Marriages

Gallup Polls reveal that less than 20 percent of Americans who get married have had any premarital counseling. And those who got such counseling are *just as likely* to divorce as those who had no marriage preparation.

For many years the Catholic Church has recognized that the main reason most marriages fail is poor communication. Most U.S. Catholic dioceses take five steps to improve communication between the man and woman who want to be married. If you are engaged, consider these steps for you and your future mate. If you are married or if you are a church leader, you can use these steps and develop an engagement preparation process for couples you know.

1. Participate in a premarital inventory. An inventory is given to help the couple objectively assess the strengths and weaknesses of their relationship. The usual format is a list of questions that force the couple to really think about areas of their lives that will later become issues of potential conflict. More detail will follow in Answer 9.

Because they're in love and agree about one or two important areas—such as religion or how many children they plan to have—couples feel that everything else will work out.

In reality, a marital inventory pulls no punches. It says without flinching if there are areas of incompatibility or issues of conflict. These issues must be resolved *before* the marriage or they will become the ammunition for the "war" to follow.

The Catholic tradition of a pre-Cana preparation for the engaged couple is a good model. Couples who are given adequate premarital counsel and work with an inventory are much more likely to avoid later conflicts.

My wife, Harriet, and I work with engaged couples in our church. We are always amazed to see how the inventory points up such differences. Many are cultural; some are religious. I recall one quiet young Asian girl who was engaged to a boisterous Italian. Whenever she went to visit his family, she felt terrible confusion and conflict because the family members were so loud and opinionated. She thought they were angry. Her background was different. When they visited her family, everyone was so subdued and quiet that her fiance felt uneasy.

The inventory also helps point out the differences in family leadership styles. Dave and Cathy came from two distinctly different homes. Dave's mom took more of a leadership role, and Dave was like his mom. Cathy, on the other hand, was more submissive. Her family tended to be individualistic, with no one person "in charge." Harriet and I told them that each needed to work on these areas. If not, their relationship would become one-sided, with Dave "taking charge" and making most of the decisions unilaterally.

In areas of communication, Dave and Cathy learned that each had different styles of sharing. Cathy liked to talk things out, discuss and review, consider and talk some more. Dave, on the other hand, said little. And when the issue was a "touchy" one, he'd clam up completely, so conflicts were never resolved.

The couple learned from the inventory that there were *many* issues on which they disagreed. They decided to work on these issues so that they could have a loving marriage relationship.

In every instance of our premarital counseling, we have been told by the couples that they were grateful for having taken the inventory. We know from personal experience that it saves marriages.

2. Establish a relationship with a mentor couple. Solidly married couples should mentor younger ones. The Catholic Church recruits couples to assist the parish priest in the premarital instruction of younger couples. The mentor couples are often called "coordinating couples," and they review an inventory with the engaged couple. The mentor couple also makes suggestions on how the engaged couple might handle the conflicts or misunderstandings the inventory brings to light.

Harriet and I have mentored fifteen young couples over the past three years. It has been and continues to be a rewarding experience. We know we have been "marriage savers" with many young couples.

We have also trained 22 mentor couples at our church who are now uniquely qualified to help engaged couples. Why? Their greatest credential is that they have marriages which have lasted an average of 30 years!

Every church has couples with solid marriages who could pass on their wisdom to younger ones. The young engaged couples benefit greatly from the experience—successes and failures—of the mature married mentor couples.

Mentor couples are the single greatest resource

churches have to save troubled marriages. Yet few older couples are ever invited to become mentors. Churches are missing out by not tapping into this unique and valuable resource.

3. Attend a weekend retreat for engaged couples. One proven retreat is Engaged Encounter. Nearly 35,000 couples attend annually.

Married couples share intimate stories with engaged couples. Then 20-25 engaged couples go into a quiet personal retreat to write reflections and share them privately with their intended spouse. The sharing is on tough questions like.

"What things do I talk to others about more easily than with you?"

"What doubts do I have in marrying you?" "What things about you make me angry?"

So intensive is Engaged Encounter that a tenth of the engagements break. Good! Better the broken engagement than the broken marriage later with two kids. More information on Engaged Encounter is included in Answer 11.

Not every church can utilize Engaged Encounter. Your church can plan an effective weekend for engaged couples using *Counsel for the Nearly and Newly Married* or *I Take Thee to be My Spouse.*

4. Participate in lectures, writing, and dialogue related to premarital issues.

Lectures and workshops can focus on such issues as how the couple will handle their money, communication, and conflict resolution. Other classes and workshops can deal with other problems newly married couples are likely to encounter.

Writing and dialogue is essential. Couples fill out workbooks sparking thought on issues that are easily ignored in the glow of romance. Often the dialogue is with other engaged couples and older, solidly married ones.

5. Spend time preparing for marriage.
Catholics typically require six months of marriage preparation from the time the couple first meets with clergy until the wedding date. In communities where religious leaders from various churches have adopted a Community Marriage Policy (see Answer 25), four-month minimum preparation is required.

The previous four steps will require time to complete. You may find that you will need more than four or six months.

Sadly, most churches have no minimum time requirement, no mentor couples, no required writing or dialogue, no retreats, no premarital inventory, and no lectures on substantive issues.

These are the elements that work! Research bears out the fact that each of these factors makes a remarkable contribution to the success of new marriages. Collectively, they will help you and your church be a marriage saver.

Biblical References
Job 12:12-13; Psalm 32:8; Isaiah 28:26; 42:16; Titus 2:1-5

Other Resources
1. *Marriage Savers* by Michael McManus (Zondervan, 1993), chapters 2-7.

2. *Marriage Savers Resource Collection,* video programs 2 and 3.

3. *Counsel for the Nearly and Newly Married* by Ernest White and James E. White (Convention Press, 1992).

4. *I Take Thee to Be My Spouse* compiled by David Apple (Convention Press, 1992).

A N S W E R   4

Insuring Marriage

Help Teenagers Abstain from Sex

Teenagers who remain chaste until they marry **reduce their odds of divorce.** Only 14 percent of virgin brides in 1980-83 were divorced by 1988; 24 percent of non-virgins had divorced. Today, less than 10 percent are virgins when they marry.

Four proven programs teach abstinence, challenge teenagers to remain sexually pure, and prepare them for marriage. True Love Waits and Why Wait? are church-based. Sex Respect and Postponing Sexual Involvement are school-based.

TRUE LOVE WAITS

The Southern Baptist Convention has pioneered a major answer to the question of teen chastity by coordinating a national campaign called True Love Waits. Between April, 1993 and July, 1994, hundreds of thousands of teenagers signed a covenant card stating:

Believing that true love waits, I make a commitment to God, myself, my family, those I date, my future mate, and my future children to remain sexually pure until the day I enter a covenant marriage relationship.

When asked why he signed a card, Julio

Hernandez, 17, said, "I just want to save myself for my future wife. I think the only gift I can give her is myself. One key reason is that I want to remain close to God. It keeps my mind free."

True Love Waits did not end with the campaign. It is now an annual emphasis promoted in churches and communities each February. You can provide True Love Waits for new youth as encouragement to teenagers who have made the commitment.

WHY WAIT?

Josh McDowell has spoken to more than eight million college students. One of his frequent themes is the need for chastity. He became suspicious about what churches were teaching youth groups about sex and conducted a Teen Sex Survey. It revealed that 75 percent of church youth in even the most conservative denominations *learned little or nothing about sex from their church*. And the study revealed that 43 percent of church youth aged 18 have had intercourse, **only slightly less than unchurched youth**.[1]

McDowell created four videos (15 minutes each) called "NO! The Positive Answer" you can use with your church youth. He tells teenagers, "God has given you rules to protect and provide for you." The video series uses humor, music, role playing, and the kids themselves speak out on the pressures, fears, and victories in the sexual arena.

SEX RESPECT

A former high school teacher, Coleen Kelly Mast, has developed an abstinence-based course now offered in several thousand high schools. In addition to the student text there is a Parent's Guide to help parents discuss this tough issue with a teen. **Parents need the help.** Only 8 percent of fathers and 15 percent of mothers have ever talked with their teen about sex.[2]

Sex Respect teaches students how to handle the "lines" they'll hear:

"You would, if you loved me!"

"If you loved me, you wouldn't ask!"

Mrs. Mast believes most sex education is "too narrow, focused only on the physical, saying if you get rid of the physical consequences of premarital sex (via contraceptives or abortion), all will be OK. That's a lie. There are serious emotional and physical effects. Even adults have difficulty getting over a sexual relationship. Teens are being taught they can act on any impulse and not have to face the consequences. How can we create a healthy society when its citizens have not learned self-control?"

The Institute for Research and Evaluation in Salt Lake City studied the long-term impact of the course and concluded: "After two years, those taking Sex Respect had pregnancy rates that were *half* of those students not in the program, but attending the same schools."

POSTPONING SEXUAL INVOLVEMENT

Postponing Sexual Involvement (PSI) is an excellent course for eighth graders in public schools.

In the 1970s, Dr. Marion Howard created a sex education program like that often found in most public schools—five classes of discussions on human sexuality, human decision-making, family planning, and contraceptives. It flopped.

Dr. Howard concluded: "Simply providing young teenagers with such information was not effective in changing sexual behavior." She also decided that the best way to reach young teens is through role models using slightly older teenagers.

These teens give information, identify pressures, and discuss problem situations. The teenage leaders produce greater and more lasting effects than adults, says Dr. Howard.

A key focus of her course is helping teenagers learn how to say "no" without hurting the others. Its premise is that young people are often pressured into doing things they really do not want to do.

To measure PSI's impact, research indicated that after a year "students who had not had PSI were as much as **five times** more likely to have initiated sex than were those who had taken it: 20 percent vs. 4 percent!" Also, the number of teen pregnancies fell by a third over a five-year period!

Biblical References
1 Corinthians 6:13-20; 10:13; 1 Thessalonians 4:3; Titus 2:11-12

Other Resources
1. **True Love Waits**, 127 Ninth Avenue North, Nashville, TN 37234. Planning kit available.
2. **Why Wait?** P.O. Box 1330, Wheaton, IL 60189 1-800-222-JOSH
3. **Sex Respect**, P.O. Box 349-M, Bradley, IL 60915.
4. **Postponing Sexual Involvement**, Box 26158, Grady Memorial Hospital, 80 Butler St. S.E., Atlanta, GA 30335.
5. *Christian Sex Education Series,* (LifeWay Press, 1993, Call 1-800-458-2772.) *Sex! What's That?* (for preadolescents) by Susan Lanford; *Sexuality: God's Gift* (for adolescents) by Ann Cannon; *Christian Sex Education: Parents and Church Leaders Guide* compiled by Jimmy Hester.
6. *Marriage Savers Resource Collection,* video program 2.
7. *Marriage Savers* by Michael McManus (Zondervan, 1993), chapter 4.

---

[1]Josh McDowell and Dick Day, *Why Wait?* (San Bernardino: Here's Life Publishers, Inc., 1987), 99.

[2]E. S. Roberts, D. Kline, and J. Cagon: *Family Life and Sexual Learning of Children, Vol 1* (Cambridge: Population Education, Inc., 1981), 32.

Insuring Marriage

Beware of Sexual Entrapments

What's wrong with sex for those in their 20s and 30s who are in love? Conventional wisdom says this is not only harmless but beneficial. However, emotional intimacy with someone other than your spouse or future spouse can lead to unfaithfulness and a lack of trust in marriage.

Harriet and I have worked as mentors to about 15 couples in recent years. "Jerry" and "Pam" had dated for four years in their early twenties, broke off for two years, and recently dated again.

We administered PREPARE, a premarital inventory in which they individually responded to 125 statements.

They scored 90 percent on their "Sexual Relationship," but 0 percent on "Religious Orientation." She was a Christian—he wasn't. They knew of that difference and were somewhat concerned about it.

However, I was puzzled by other answers. On the statement, "We have discussed the responsibilities of a father in raising children," Jerry marked "Agree." Pam marked "Disagree." I asked him to explain his answer. He said. "We *have* discussed the role of a father in raising children."

Pam broke in, "We have *not* discussed it to the point of making a decision."

Jerry replied, "We've discussed things like who'll watch the children. She says she wants to stay home and not work. I feel that to survive, we have to have two incomes. We'll have to put the kids in day care. If you live in northern Virginia, it will be too expensive without two incomes."

Pam was dumbfounded—on two levels. First, this was hardly a *discussion* of the role of the father in bringing up children. It was more of a *declaration* by Jerry. Secondly, she was hearing— much more clearly than ever before—Jerry's absolute denial of her being a stay-at-home mom.

Trying to mediate, I said, "You don't have to live in northern Virginia to do your kind of work. You could live in Lynchburg."

"Lynchburg?" he asked.

"In Lynchburg, you could buy a home for $60,000, and Pam could be a stay-at-home mom," I explained. It was a point of view he did not want to consider.

"It's unrealistic. I work at three jobs now. I can't imagine making a mortgage payment with one income."

Pam's brow furrowed. She was hearing something from him on this issue that she had not heard before. Finally, Harriet got suspicious, and asked, "Jerry, do you really want to have children?"

He leaned back, looked down and said, "No— not particularly."

My eyes darted over to Pam. Her mouth dropped in shock and horror. She'd never heard that he did not want to be a father before. But why not? They'd gone together for nearly *five years*—how could they not talk about it?

The answer is that they were 90 percent compatible on sexual issues. Pam, although a Christian, had given in to the pressure and became sexually active with Jerry. And it became a trap.

Instead of talking through key issues about their relationship, sex gave them the illusion of intimacy. Yet it prevented them from really understanding each other.

Pam was wasting her time with such a person. He was hostile to her faith and wouldn't go to church with her. As is true in so many cases, Pam made the mistake of thinking she could change Jerry. Instead of spending nearly five years with Jerry, she would have been better off going to a church with a strong singles group where she might have met a Christian man who shared her values.

Sex before marriage is a trap that fools one (or both) of the partners into thinking they have a closeness and intimacy that will make the relationship work. But it's merely a facade. **Intimacy is more than a sexual relationship. Chastity before marriage is a proven way to avoid divorce**.

If you find yourself in this entrapment, seek counsel from your pastor, a counselor, a mentor couple, or a Christian friend. If you recognize a dating couple that may be in this entrapment, share your concern. Chastity before marriage is a proven way to avoid divorce.

Biblical References
1 Corinthians 6:13-20; 1 Thessalonians 4:3; Hebrews 4:15,.16; James 1:12

Other Resources
1. *Marriage Savers* by Michael McManus (Zondervan, 1993), chapter 5.

2. *Marriage Savers Resource Collection:* "Helping Singles and Seriously Dating Couples."

A N S W E R   6

Insuring Marriage

Don't Live Together in a Trial Marriage

Fearing a divorce, millions of seriously dating couples have begun "trial marriages" in which they live together but are not married. Cohabitation is particularly common among children of divorce.

In March 1970, the Census Bureau reported that 523,000 unmarried couples were living together. By 1993 the number soared to 3.5 million couples.

How many marriages are preceded by a period where the couples simply live together? The University of Wisconsin's *National Survey of Families and Households* estimates that only 8 percent of first marriages were preceded by cohabitation in the late 1960s, but more than half were preceded by cohabitation by 1990.

In remarriage (where one or both parties have been divorced), **two-thirds** lived together first.

The *National Survey of Families and Households* reports that cohabiting couples face two facts:

1. At least one person in 90 percent of the couples wants to marry, but 40 percent of the couples who live together *break up before marriage* after about 1.3 years.

Many then suffer from "premarital divorce." Still, they are likely to try living with Partner B, then C, and end up at age 37 wondering why they're not married.

The result: never-married Americans have **doubled** from 21 million people in 1970 to 42 million by 1992.

2. Marriages that are preceded by living together have 50 percent higher disruption rates (divorce or separation) than marriages without premarital cohabitation according to the *National Survey of Families and Households*. The normal divorce rate is about 50 percent. Thus, those who live in a "trial marriage" first face a 75 percent divorce rate after 10 years![1]

Marriage is not a shoe one can try on before buying it!

But for millions, for whom *cohabitation has become a substitute for a covenant marriage*, they've encountered a disease that kills the marriage at the front end of the relationship. And it's a disease that spreads to affect matrimony for those who marry *after* living together.

The answer is plain: **Do not cohabit!** If you are living with someone, consider the odds. If you know of a couple living in a trial marriage, share with them the odds. Of 100 couples who begin a trial marriage, 40 don't marry. Of 60 couples who do wed, there are 45 divorces after 10 years. That's an *85 percent failure rate*.

With a mere 15 percent chance of success, why do young people, especially Christian couples, consider relationships that disregard Scripture? Paul was succinct: "Flee from sexual immorality" (1 Cor. 6:18). Hebrews 13:4 is also clear: "Marriage should be honored by all and the marriage bed be kept pure, for God will judge the adulterer and all the sexually immoral."

Fortunately, there is a better way for seriously dating couples to structure their relationship. Instead of an 85 percent failure rate after they marry, as with cohabitation, God's plan gives *a 90 percent chance of success*!

Biblical References
Romans 6:1-2, 14; 1 Corinthians 6:13-20; 2 Corinthians 5:17; Galatians 5:16,17; Hebrews 13:4

Other Resources
1. *Marriage Savers* by Michael McManus (Zondervan, 1993), chapters 2 and 5.
2. *Marriage Savers Resource Collection,* video program 2.

---

[1]Larry Bumpass, *National Survey of Families and Households* Working Papers #2 and #5, Center for Demography and Ecology at the University of Wisconsin, 1989.

A N S W E R 7

Insuring
Marriage

Seriously Dating Couples Can Avoid Mistakes

If cohabitation is the worst step that seriously dating couples can take, what is the best step? Consider Relationship Instruction, developed by Dr. Jim A. Talley, a former pastor and presently a marital therapist who has worked with over 13,000 single adults over a 24 year period. Relationship Instruction is the best way for couples who are not yet engaged to be sure they've chosen the right mate.

Look at the results. Since 1976, thousands of couples have signed the Relationship Instruction contract. Talley reports that fewer than 10 percent gave up and did not complete it. And, of all the seriously dating couples who did complete it, half of them did not marry. But of those who did marry, *less than 10 percent* have ended in divorce or separation. Relationship Instruction is "marriage insurance."

The demands of Relationship Instruction may seem unusual—even intimidating. The couple signs a contract—called the "Pre-requisites"—agreeing to specific, serious steps to promote spiritual maturity in Christ; build trust; develop agape love; and learn to control physical, emotional, and mental habits.

Requirements include:

- Read *Too Close Too Soon*
- Complete weekly workbook assignments.
- Complete an eight-session, four-month course (even if the relationship breaks up).
- Do not discuss an engagement.
- Do not date anyone else.
- Limit time together.
- Avoid sexual activity (to the point of calling the instructor or mentor couple if they exceed French kissing.)

The following is one area of a couple's relationship that is considered. The control of sexual activity is important in evaluating a relationship. If you are in a seriously dating relationship, complete this exercise.

HOW FAR?

If you are in a seriously dating relationship, circle the number that represents the highest level of physical involvement between you and your friend in the last 30 days.

1 Look
2 Touch
3 Lightly holding hands
4 Constantly holding hands
5 Light kiss
6 Strong kiss
7 French kiss
8 Fondling breasts
9 Fondling sexual organs
10 Sexual intercourse

If you circled number seven or higher, seriously consider where your physical involvement is taking you in your relationship.

Harriet and I have used Relationship Instruction over the years. We received a call one Saturday. "We went further than we should have last night," said Dave. "We're disappointed in ourselves, but we feel better about calling you. It's good that our church holds us accountable."

How do couples generally react to Relationship Instruction? "First, we have needed someone to be accountable to," said Cathy. "Second, the workbook gave us something concrete to do. For Dave to read my thoughts on paper meant that I had to be vulnerable."

Dave commented, "When you see it written down on paper, it seems more serious." He discovered by writing out his goals that he'd like to have his own business in five years. So he decided to do some free-lance work on Saturdays, to see if he could find the clients he'd need in order to go on his own.

Cathy added, "I feel sorry for the couples who don't go through this kind of preparation before marriage."

Another couple, Gary and Janine agreed. "Relationship Instruction helped us pace the relationship," says Gary. "Sexual discipline made my commitment more real to my partner. By (our) abstaining, she learned to trust me more."

Janine added, "It gave me a way to understand the person I was romantically inclined toward. I got a more objective picture of his likes, dislikes, what goals we have in common, what our financial situation was, our future as far as children."

Andrea, a divorcee who married twice-divorced Bob, said "It helped us put on the brakes. People who've been married before can easily jump the hurdles of the heart stuff and head into the physical part."

Bob adds "I had serious doubts . . . after two failures, I needed help to prepare for marriage."

These couples discovered that Relationship Instruction was a wonderful investment in building their relationship.

Biblical References
Deuteronomy 4:29; 29:9; Hosea 10:12; Philippians 4:9; Hebrews 11:6; James 1:5, 6

Other Resources
1. For information and to order Relationship Instruction workbooks and *Too Close Too Soon,* call 1-800-645-3761.

2. *Marriage Savers Resource Collection,* video program 2.

3. *Marriage Savers* by Michael McManus (Zondervan, 1993), chapters 5 and 6.

A N S W E R   8

Insuring Marriage

Learn from a Relationship That Doesn't Lead to Marriage

What if, despite your investment in Relationship Instruction, you learn there are still too many areas of incompatibility and your relationship falls apart? What happens if this process does not lead to marriage? Is there still a value in taking the course? Yes!

Half those taking Relationship Instruction do not marry—but **learn about themselves** and **how to build a future relationship.**

Consider "Liz" and "Sam," another couple we mentored, both of whom were in their 40s but had never married.

Sam explained his approach to women in nautical terms: "I love to take a woman out in my boat for a sail. Inevitably a little squall kicks up—an argument—and I think, 'She must not be God's person for me.' So I take her 'back to the dock.' But I finally realized I've been taking women back to the dock for 20 years. It's time I learned how to sail with one out of the harbor. And Relationship Instruction seems like a perfect way to do it."

The contractual nature of the course gave Liz a great sense of hope and freedom. For a year she'd been afraid of intimacy. "In our relationship," she said, "it was a monologue by him. He talked and I listened. It never became a dialogue until we started this process. Only then did I feel free to express myself."

And boy, did she ever! When Sam got to work on Monday he checked his "phone mail." There was Liz, with a 30 minute monologue on their relationship. "I was still afraid to say what I was feeling to him face to face, but I could do it on voice mail because I wasn't worried that he'd leave."

That happened several times, and Sam did feel like putting her "back on the dock," but he'd made the four-month commitment, and he honored it.

That summer Liz felt like getting out of the relationship, but she didn't. Later, it was Sam's turn to say he wanted out.

Harriet and I advised both of them to stop seeing each other for a few months. "You may find that there is a hole in your life that only she can fill," I told Sam. "But give her, and yourself, some space and time." They both agreed.

In the final session, we asked them "**What was the value of the course?**"

"First, it is a way of learning about yourself. Relationship Instruction gives a focus, and it definitely develops some communication skills," Liz told me. "Also, we were not really friends before, per se. If we had married, it would have been difficult. There was no foundation. Relationship Instruction showed us how to develop a relationship. Out of that we are becoming good friends, which is necessary in marriage"

Curiously, Sam came to similar conclusions. "I took the course because we wanted to learn about ourselves. This was the deepest sharing I have ever had with another person in my life. That's both the greatest and the scariest thing."

While the relationship did not work out, both of them grew. They learned they could build a deep relationship with another person—an important first for each of them. They emerged with not just a high respect for each other—but a much higher self-respect. By keeping the sexual element sharply limited, they can in clear conscience walk away from the relationship, feeling good about themselves and the other person.

Ten Steps in Working Through a Broken Relationship

Step 1   Deal with your emotions.

Step 2   Forgive yourself.

Step 3   Forgive the other person.

Step 4   Do not date for three to six months minimum to allow your emotions time to heal.

Step 5   Be cautious about entering into a long-term commitment with someone else.

Step 6   Get involved helping others.

Step 7   Treat yourself to something special.

Step 8   If negative emotions continue, seek help from a counselor or your pastor.

Step 9   Build same-sex friendships.

Step 10   Participate regularly in church and community activities.

Biblical References

Psalm 138:8; Proverbs 3:4-6; Isaiah 28:26; Philippians 1:9; 1 Thessalonians 4:1; 2 Timothy 1:7; 3:14-16;

Other Resources

1. *Marriage Savers Resource Collection,* video program 2.

2. *Marriage Savers* by Michael McManus (Zondervan, 1993), chapters 5 and 6.

ANSWER 9

Insuring Marriage

Use a Premarital Inventory to Identify Strengths and Weaknesses

Dr. James Dobson in *Love For a Lifetime* writes: "A dating relationship is designed to conceal information, not reveal it. Each partner puts his or her best foot forward, hiding embarrassing facts, habits, flaws, and temperaments."[1]

Fortunately, there are ways to cut through those facades. A premarital inventory has the ability to predict marital success or failure *in time to do something about it.*

One of the best inventories is called PREPARE. It consists of 125 questions, asked of the man and woman separately. Their answers are compared by computer and returned to a qualified interpreter.

The man and woman indicate whether they agree or disagree with statements like:

I believe that most disagreements we currently have will decrease after marriage.

I am concerned about my partner's drinking and/or smoking.

I can easily share my positive and negative feelings with my partner.

I wish my partner were more careful in spending money.

Each person is asked about the other person. What surfaces is a virtual X-ray of the relationship. Ten questions are asked in each of a dozen areas (finances, conflict resolution, sex, and differences in family background). The results tell if the couple agrees or disagrees on each question.

The inventory then gives the couple an objective and realistic assessment of their relative "Relationship Strengths" or "Growth Areas."

Harriet and I administered PREPARE to Dave, a journalist, and Cathy, an attractive nurse. They had known each other for nearly two years. Cathy was surprised that a simple questionnaire could probe the unexplored areas of their relationship.

In the evaluation, counselors focus first on the couple's "relationship strengths." So, we congratulated Cathy and Dave for their 90 percent agreement on religious orientation. But I noted that on "conflict resolution" they only scored 30 percent.

PREPARE goes beyond merely pointing out problems. Counselors are urged to help the couple find their own solutions by focusing on an issue and leading the couple through steps to resolve conflict. Learning how to resolve their conflicts is as important as the objective assessment of discovering what their areas of conflict are.

Successful marriages are built on good communication and conflict resolution skills. And the good news is these skills can be taught.

I tested that thesis by asking Dave and Cathy to define their current problem of conflict resolution.

Cathy said there were times she "gets the silent treatment" when she brings up a problem. Or Dave will say something "is fine" when he's really putting her off.

Dave replied, "I need time to think. Sometimes I am not sure what to say. She has about 1,000 words on a subject, while I have about 50. She wears me out."

I asked, "How do you each contribute to the problem?"

Cathy said, "When he clams up on me, I put my answering machine on and don't take his call, even if I am home."

"So you give *him* the silent treatment!" I commented. She smiled.

Harriet and I asked for solutions tried in the past that were not successful. Next, we asked them to list all the possible solutions. They discussed these and other ideas, agreed on a combination of them, then decided what each should do to work toward a solution.

"That was a wall in our relationship," said Dave later, "and you gave us a stepladder over that wall."

Of 100,000 couples who take PREPARE annually, some 10,000 couples—a tenth—find so many problems, they actually decide to break their engagements.

But better a broken engagement than a broken marriage.

Those who do break their engagements invariably have such bad scores that they'd have probably divorced if they had gotten married.

A premarital inventory like PREPARE actually *helps couples avoid a bad marriage before it even begins!*

We were mentors of one couple who appeared to be "in love." But their scores ranged from 0 to only 30 percent. When we called them up to say we were ready to give them their results, the young woman told us, "We broke our engagement after we discussed PREPARE. I was nervous about the relationship, but this convinced me it would not work."

"You did the right thing," I replied.

There is another value of PREPARE. It provides a way for a mentor couple to relate to a couple and give them suggestions on how they might solve some of their conflicts.

Harriet and I are not professionals in marriage counseling, but in 29 years of marriage, we've learned to deal with conflict and other problems that threaten a relationship.

If you are getting married soon, or know a couple who is, and you do not know anyone who is trained to administer an inventory, contact the people at PREPARE/ENRICH. There are 25,000 pastors and counselors trained to administer the inventory. Ask for the name of someone in your area who is trained to offer the one-day seminar.

Biblical References
Deuteronomy 7:12; Job 36:11; Psalm 25:9; 37:4; James 1:5

Other Resources
1. **PREPARE/ENRICH**, Box 190, Minneapolis, MN 55440.

2. *Marriage Savers* by Michael McManus (Zondervan, 1993), chapter 6.

3. *Marriage Savers Resource Collection,* videos programs 2 and 3.

---

[1]James C. Dobson, *Love for a Lifetime* (Portland: Multnomah, 1987), 22.

Insuring Marriage

Help Insure and Save Marriages by Being a Mentor Couple

The greatest untapped resource to insure and save marriages are **married couples who can act as mentors for younger couples.** If you have been married 20-50 years, you have much to offer. You've learned the secrets of successful marriage. As a result, you hold a great store of wisdom and experience.

These couples know how to communicate, resolve conflict, and cherish one another. Young couples would love to tap their wisdom.

Solidly married couples are a treasure that can be found in the pews of any church. Yet very few churches have considered inviting them to mentor engaged or seriously dating couples.

Catholic churches are the exception. For 15-plus years, older couples have been mentoring engaged couples. These mentors, or "coordinating couples," work in one of three ways, beginning with the most useful and intensive interventions.

1. Engaged Encounter. Mentor couples donate a weekend of time to lead a group of engaged couples in an intensive retreat. This is by far the best experience for the engaged couples, but also the most demanding for the married couples in terms of energy and time.

2. Evenings For the Engaged. Typically, mentor couples give three evenings of time to ask probing questions. They also share their own experience with the engaged couple.

One mentor explained: "One after another is shocked by what their fiancés are saying: 'What do you mean, we will spend Christmas at *your* folks' house? Who says *you* will manage the checkbook?' Clearly, tough issues had not been faced by many couples until they were asked probing questions. By the third evening, all the couples love the experience because they are learning so much. After the weddings, many keep in contact with us. They feel they have someone they can turn to if they get in trouble. It has been a very satisfying experience."

3. Pre-Cana Workshops. Pre-Cana Workshops are three all-day Saturday sessions. Engaged couples must write in workbooks, read each other's comments and talk about them with each other—perhaps with a table of three other engaged couples led by a mentor couple.

OUR MENTORING MODEL

Harriet and I have fashioned a different mentoring model at our church. We have trained 22 couples whose marriages have lasted an average of 30 years. They work with seriously dating and engaged couples on a one-to-one basis. Our mentors also meet with one couple privately in their home and administer the PREPARE inventory. When the computerized report is returned, the mentors go over the results with their assigned couple in two or three sessions in their home.

Mentor training includes having the mentor couple take an ENRICH inventory, which raises many of the same issues as PREPARE. This strengthens the mentor couple as well as trains them to work with engaged couples.

The Mentor's View

Mentors seem to find a new appreciation of Jesus' admonition, "Give and it will be given to you" (Luke 6:38).

Mentor Ted Kupelian said, "Of the 12 years I've served as a leader, we've enjoyed it as much as anything. The two of us working as a couple has made it the most rewarding work."

Bob Stenstrom, another mentor, said that PRE-PARE was "very helpful to our couple. The feedback was the gist of our two sessions together and a good springboard to a number of other issues. It supports sharing our own experiences without being pontifical or pious. It was invaluable in developing the insights into their burgeoning relationship."

Joe Ann Stenstrom, Bob's wife of 30-plus years, added, "In our experience of being a mentor couple, one of the best parts is getting to know your own relationship. It forces you to analyze what makes your husband-wife relationship work. In taking the (ENRICH) inventory, it confirmed some of our own areas of compatibility—and differences that keep life interesting. *It shows why you got married in the first place!"*

Reactions of the Engaged

"Very valuable experience," wrote one young groom-to-be in an evaluation. "PREPARE and mentoring are so good that all those planning to marry should be required by law to take this course!"

"The highlight of the course was the mentoring," said Roberto Anson. "Bob and Joe Ann Stenstrom were fantastic. I heard their wisdom and saw how they functioned as a team. Through them and PRE-PARE I learned a lot."

Hugh, another mentor, said, "The engaged see that we're open and willing to be vulnerable, and tell them about our private life. That, in turn, allows them to open up more of themselves."

Mentoring in Perspective

A pastor cannot usually do all the premarital counseling in his church. Also, it's valuable to have both a male and a female perspective. Harriet is always sensitive to emotional issues that escape me. And I pick up on male frustrations she doesn't see. I tend to pay attention to the *ideas* being expressed, but she picks up on the *feelings* and body language, every bit as important as verbal communication.

The apostle Paul said the job of the pastor is "to prepare God's people for works of service" (Eph. 4:12). What more important service is there than being a marriage saver?

Biblical References
Isaiah 30:21; Philippians 1:9; 3:14-16; 1 Thessalonians 4:1

Other Resources
1. *Marriage Savers* by Michael McManus (Zondervan, 1993), chapter 7.

2. *Marriage Savers Resource Collection,* video programs 2, 3, and 4.

A N S W E R   1 1

Insuring Marriage

Participate in a Premarital Retreat to Improve Communication Skills

Since three-fifths of all divorces are the result of poor communication, the best step you can take before the wedding ceremony to improve your communication skills is to attend a weekend retreat for engaged couples. Your church can develop a weekend retreat using resources like *Counsel for the Nearly and Newly Married,* or *Communication and Intimacy: Covenant Marriage.* Or, invite an effective conference leader to train couples.

Or you can attend Engaged Encounter, an intensive weekend retreat developed by Catholics, and since adopted by mainline and evangelical Protestant churches. The aim of Engaged Encounter is "to reduce the number of potential divorces, strengthen family ties, and reaffirm the biblical notion of covenant."

Its motto is: **"A wedding is but a day, but a marriage is for a lifetime."**

Engaged Encounter begins with a presentation of views of what a Christian marriage ought to be. After the presentation, each engaged couple is asked to go off together and write answers to some questions, read each other's reflections, then discuss them in private. The couples are asked to answer some tough questions:

"What about you makes me angry?"

"What doubts do I have in marrying you?"

"What differences between us might cause a problem if not discussed now—temperaments, children, past relationships, etc.?"

Challenging questions! But necessary ones.

This pattern repeats itself on other topics such as "Openness and Communication" and "Signs of a Closed Relationship."

More questions and private talk follow.

"How do I feel about committing myself to loving you 100 percent for the rest of my life?"

"How is God working in our engagement?"

"How will we reflect God's love after our wedding?"

All of that is covered before lunch on Saturday! Later the engaged couples focus on the myriad of practical decisions in marriage: whether to have children, when, how many, and how to discipline them.

Another session focuses on "Sex and Sexuality." A biblical perspective on sex as a gift from God leads to a talk on how to be unselfish and giving.

In "Plan of Life," money issues are covered:

"Who pays the bills?"

"How much money will go into savings?"

"What is the desired role of prayer to your long-term goals?"

On Saturday night this intensity is relieved with an informal dialogue between all couples on some hot questions:

"Is premarital sex a sin?"

"How important is sex in marriage?"

"What if my mate is unfaithful?"

On Sunday morning the couples discuss "Forgiveness in Marriage" or "How to Share Vulnerability."

The weekend closes with a joyous time of worship and communion.

Reactions?

"This weekend showed me I have a lot of fears, mistrust, and difficulties risking honesty first with myself and then with my fiancé. It made me realize that commitment and love are things I have never taken seriously before," said one participant.

"It was a painful, emotional, draining, tearful, joyful, releasing, and finally peaceful experience," said one woman.

What engaged couple would not want to have a focused weekend in preparing for marriage? Plan one for your church or find out how to attend an Engaged Encounter weekend near you.

Biblical References

Leviticus 25:17; Proverbs 15:33; Matthew 18:4; 23:12; Colossians 3:9-10, 12-15

Other Resources

1. For more information on Engaged Encounter:

Protestants: Call Dave and Sue Edwards (303) 753-9407.

Catholics: Call Dave and Millie Florijan (412) 487-5116.

2. *Marriage Savers* by Michael McManus (Zondervan, 1993), chapter 7.

3. *Marriage Savers Resource Collection,* video program 3.

A N S W E R   1 2

Invest Time and Energy in Marriage Preparation

Engaged couples should seek out the most rigorous marriage preparation to insure having the same mate for life.

Recently Harriet and I went to a friend's wedding. The service and reception were wonderful. Don was as handsome as the bride was beautiful.

But nine days before the wedding Don called to ask about PREPARE. I explained how useful the inventory was, and how we use it to mentor young couples. Don asked, "How long does it take to get the results?"

"About 10 days," I replied. "They're sent to Minneapolis for computer scoring, then they're returned."

He then asked, "Can you hand score the answers, rather than have it sent off?"

"No. Why do you ask?"

"Well, I'm getting married in just nine days, and feel shaky about it, to be honest." What a time to feel shaky! I'd talked to Don six weeks earlier, and urged him then to take PREPARE. I sent him my book, *Marriage Savers,* but he hadn't looked at it until now and he began to panic.

In reading about PREPARE, Don realized that he should have taken it as a way to be sure that he had chosen the right woman, as well as for an objective assessment of the strengths and weaknesses of their relationship.

"Twice my pastor encouraged me to postpone the wedding," Don confessed. That was a red flag. His pastor, who knew them both, felt they were rushing into marriage.

I told Don that they could either take PREPARE before the wedding, and have the results after the honeymoon, or when they got back they could take ENRICH, a similar inventory—for married couples—that measures marriage satisfaction and relational compatibility.

Needless to say, neither step would help a person like Don who wasn't sure about getting married in nine days. What if their scores were poor? A tenth of couples who take PREPARE break their engagements, thus avoiding a bad marriage before it begins.

The trouble is, as almost every pastor will testify, it's extremely difficult to convince couples who have set a wedding date to invest time and energy in marriage preparation. Maybe one (or both) of them is afraid such a step might threaten their wedding.

Therefore, it seems a bit idealistic to expect the couple to give this matter priority unless there is a standard.

Both churches and the state should demand a minimum time and a number of certain prescribed steps of marriage preparation before couples can marry.

Sound radical? Not at all. Remember that most Catholic dioceses require *six months* of marriage preparation, and communities adopting Community Marriage Policies are requiring a minimum of *four months*. That six months can be filled with premarital testing, work with a mentor couple, a weekend retreat, and classes and lectures. That time ensures reality to penetrate romance.

In America, engagements are most often looked at as merely a time to plan for a wedding and a honeymoon. This is naive.

Engagements are a proven time to test a relationship to see if it has the resiliency to last for a lifetime. Preparation should be rigorous.

If you are planning a wedding for yourself or involved with one for a family member or friend, it is important that time be taken for preparation.

Yet we know that marriage preparation is a weak link. Couples do not think seriously enough about this need. That is why we should help them by making such preparation *mandatory.*

Engaged couples need to search for the most rigorous marriage preparation programs. If it's not possible to find such a program in a church in your community, couples should seek out a demanding marriage preparation inventory and workbook.

Biblical References
Psalm 32:8; Isaiah 2:3; Proverbs 6:23; Hebrews 4:12; James 1:5, 21-25

Other Resources
1. *Marriage Savers* by Michael McManus (Zondervan, 1993), chapters 6 and 12.

2. *Marriage Savers Resource Collection,* video program 3.

3. *Counsel for the Nearly and Newly Married,* by Ernest White and James E. White (Convention Press, 1993).

4. *Before You Say "I Do": Study Manual,* by W. Roberts and N. Wright (Harvest House, 1978).

A N S W E R   1 3

Insuring Marriage

Newlyweds Can Learn to Resolve Conflict

After six months of marriage, half of all couples witness dramatic increases in the frequency of arguments. They're often surprised at how critical they have become of their mate. Doubts emerge. They wonder *if they really married the right person.*

Before the wedding, in the glow of romance, everyone's mate is "perfect." After the wedding, often on the honeymoon, disenchantment creeps in. One of the partners gets upset, put down, or has feelings hurt. Soon, one or both of the partners feel "trapped" by their marriage.

Eventually, though, couples can reach maturity. Things finally smooth out for them—or else they go on to separation and divorce!

How can couples, caught in the sudden horror of this disenchantment, be helped to discover this maturity? Harriet and I faced such a specific case.

Heather and Peter asked to sit in our class. They had been married three months. Heather had a quiet sadness about her that seemed unusual for a newlywed. Peter was aloof and impatient.

We suggested that they take ENRICH, the marital inventory similar to PREPARE. "The biggest thing I've encountered is a lack of communication,"

Heather told us. ENRICH turned out to be an X-ray of their relationship. In 6 of 13 areas surveyed, their scores were only 10 to 20 percent in agreement.

We began our interpretation of their scores by praising relationship strengths. "One area of real strength in your marriage is your agreement on basic religious questions. For example, since you both feel your faith is important to your relationship, you can use it to help you bridge problems. When you argue, stop and pray for wisdom.

"But in communication, Heather, you say you're afraid to tell your partner what you think or ask him for what you want. Yet Peter wishes you were more willing to share your feelings with him. Your score says you both have serious arguments over unimportant issues."

We discussed their communication techniques, then I observed an area of conflict. "Peter, you wish she was more thrifty. And you see a substance abuse issue. What do you mean by that?" Peter referred to Heather's smoking problem.

"That's not a problem," Heather snapped. "Sure . . . sometimes I have a cigarette, but not more than *once every two weeks.*"

I said, "Well, this seems to be an area of conflict. How do you resolve your conflicts?"

"We both get frustrated," Peter sighed. He looked at Heather, and barked, "And you *are* driven to smoke. "

They said many of their conflicts were over money, a typical area of dispute among newlyweds. Peter owned an old home but had let it run down. Heather was trying to fix it up. But Peter thought she was spending too much money and time on it. She was hurt because "all he does is criticize." She added, "You express your feelings but always get shot down, so you don't want to share again."

They asked how Harriet and I argued. I replied, "Our relationship is always more important than the issue in dispute, so we want to be in consensus on any decision, especially involving money."

Harriet added, "If we can't resolve an issue, we'll just postpone making a decision about it."

I asked them to describe their areas of conflict. Peter replied, "I go off to work and get beat up at work, but Heather doesn't have that aggravation. She doesn't have a job—which we agree on—but all of her friends from school are 'breeding' and she's got a book she wants to write—"

Heather interrupted. "Wait a minute! *I have been hugely busy.* I'm working on the other house, still have thank-you notes from the wedding to write." Then she paused. "But he's right about the book. What I have in mind is a Christian book." Heather's eyes began to sparkle as she shared her dream of writing. "My mother's closest friend has written 'conversations with Jesus' and I'd—"

Peter interrupted her this time. "That's just my point. I kill myself at work but lose respect for her when she uses all her time on errands and little things that don't matter, then doesn't work on the good things. I'm working hard to free her to do work that we both believe to be important and creative. I mean, she's good at writing—she shouldn't be doing all these petty little things."

Finally. Here was the source of his anger. But now his anger was controlled and as he spoke, Heather was hearing his point of view as for the first time. She watched him with affection as she witnessed his love and respect for her.

"He's never said that before," she said softly. "He's right. I really *do* want to write. It combines three loves of my life—things of God, words, and the things dear to me. But I guess I've been procrastinating . . ." It was a special moment. From that point I knew they'd be successful in working out their disputes.

Heather turned to Harriet and me. "I'm taking

Peter's words to me as God giving me encouragement and admonition, and I want you two to help me be accountable."

Heather smiled, "This has been a wonderful evening." Gently, we pushed them out the door at 1:00 a.m. Their three-year marriage is doing well.

There are proven answers! First, ENRICH "shined a light on our relationship," as Heather said.

But the inventory would be useless unless the issues surfaced with another couple. A mature married couple can take the time to explore in depth examples from real life. A newlywed couple can more readily identify with the mentor couple. There is the sense that this couple has faced similar struggles and came through them successfully.

Use ENRICH and become a mentor couple. Any church that trains mentor couples to use PREPARE with seriously dating couples is already training those mentors to use ENRICH.

You can even continue to mentor the same couples you helped prepare for marriage.

Biblical References
Psalm 51:6; Proverbs 6:23; Matthew 7:24-25; James 1:2-4; 5:16

Other Resources
1. *Marriage Savers* by Michael McManus (Zondervan, 1993), chapter 8.

2. *Marriage Savers Resource Collection*, video program 4.

3. *I Take Thee as My Spouse*, compiled by David Apple (Convention Press, 1992).

4. *Covenant Marriage: Partnership and Commitment* by Diana Garland and Betty Hassler (LifeWay Press, 1989).

5. *Communication and Intimacy: Covenant Marriage* by Gary Chapman and Betty Hassler, (LifeWay Press, 1992).

A N S W E R 1 4

Insuring Marriage

Husband, Love Your Wife; Wife, Love Your Husband

Scripture contains principles for building a lifelong marriage. Memorize and apply them in your marriage relationship.

My brother, Tim, asked me to read the famous passage on love from 1 Corinthians 13 at his wedding. Later, he gave me the opportunity to say a few words from my heart. "Our culture says that *love is a feeling*. But Scripture defines *love as a decision,* an act of the will. Are you naturally patient? I'm not. I'm impatient. By nature I am naturally self-seeking, and easily angered. To be anything different takes an act of will on my part, and the help of God," I said.

"So, if I am to love Harriet, I must deny my natural feelings, and *decide* to be patient, to seek her good before mine, to hold my temper with her. I fall short, but I do a much better job cultivating these virtues with her now than when we married 28 years ago.

"And I've learned that when I take Paul's advice to *show* love, my *feeling* of love increases."

Too many say, "I don't love her (or him) any more. The feeling isn't there any more." My answer is simple—then **do something to show love**, and your feeling of love will return. Especially for men, feelings follow actions.

WHAT DOES SCRIPTURE SAY ABOUT LOVE IN MARRIAGE?

• Ephesians 5:21: "Submit to one another out of reverence for Christ."

In God's eyes, **the man and the woman are of equal importance**. Too many men quote verse 22 "Wives, submit to your husbands."—out of context, forgetting what was said in verse 21, that submission should be mutual. **Neither partner is superior or inferior. However, the partners have different roles**.

• Ephesians 5:22: "Wives, submit to your husbands."

That doesn't mean that wives are supposed to be doormats and have no position of importance. Rather, submission is a conscious decision to act in a loving way to your partner.

Looking again at 1 Corinthians 13, we're reminded that **the expected behavior is love**. But the modern view is flawed, often self-serving—"If you do this for me, I'll love you." There are strings attached. Biblical love is unconditional.

• Ephesians 5:23: "For the husband is the head of the wife as Christ is head of the church."

"The husband does this by *leading, loving, and caring*" according to David Sunde, speaker at a Family Life Conference of Campus Crusade for Christ. He also said: "We are accountable to God for our wives and children."

Leading

In the area of sex, Sunde asked if husbands had ever taken the lead and asked their wives, "How is your sex life?" 1 Corinthians 7:4 says, "The husband's body does not belong to him alone but also to his wife."

Sunde continued, "Leadership involves managing your home. Do you have spiritual goals for your family, beyond going to church on Sunday? Do you have goals for your wife's intellectual development? That is leadership—setting goals." Men can take the responsibility to lead family devotions and go with the family to church and Sunday School.

I recall on another occasion Rev. Rick Yoder saying he once had a distressed call from a mother about her disruptive five-year-old son who bullied others. He agreed to see her, but told her to leave the boy at home and bring the father.

Yoder turned to the father and asked, "Do you spend much time with your son?" He said, "My job is very demanding." Yoder replied, "You played football in college. Have you ever thrown a football to your son? Who disciplines him?"

His wife began to sob, "Honey, I can't carry this burden any longer. I need help. I need you to take responsibility." So Yoder gave him two assignments: "Your son needs to spend time with his dad. And you send a note to the teacher saying you'll hold the son accountable for poor behavior."

A navy captain once told me, "I've let my job run away with my time, 80 hours a week. My perspective on the priority of my family has changed. I am going to schedule time for Christ and my family."

Loving

Sunde recalled that one day his wife asked, "David, why do you love me?"

He thought, "I need to work on taxes. I don't need this now." But instead he said, "I love you because the Bible says, 'Husbands, love your wives.' " She was disappointed.

Often, no sacrifice is required to show love, only thoughtfulness. One winter, Sunde cut a rose and brought it to his wife, saying, "Here is the last rose of the season for you."

She glowed, "You really love me!"

Caring

Ephesians 5:28-29 says, "Husbands ought to love their wives as their own bodies. He who loves his wife loves himself. After all, no one ever hated his own body, but he feeds and cares for it, just as Christ does the church."

Sunde said he often asks husbands, "What are your wife's greatest concerns?"

Most men get embarrassed, and admit, "I don't know."

He replies, "Caring is expressed when *she knows she is your priority.* Your wife should be the number one priority on your schedule."

Husbands and Wives Are to Love Each Other

Both partners in a marriage can learn from this model. Men, as well as women, need to be more loving and kind, more forgiving of their partner. True forgiveness may mean the complete surrender of our "rights" in order to rebuild a relationship.

The marriage process of "two becoming one" (Gen. 2:24) does not happen easily or automatically. It takes work. And it has to involve *tolerance*— the art of seeing things from the other's point of view.

Jay Kesler, in his book, *Restoring a Loving Marriage,* says, "Love is behavior, and it is possible to restore love by acting in obedience to God. . . . Only those who commit to trying harder will survive."[1]

When there is **mutual love** and a concern for the well-being of the other partner, both husbands and wives will discover the marriage that God intended for them.

Biblical References

Matthew 10:39; Mark 9:35; 1 Corinthians 13; Ephesians 5:18-25; Colossians 3:17-19; Hebrews 12:1-4; 1 John 4:18-20

Other Resources

1. *Quiet Times for Couples,* by H. Norman Wright (Harvest House Publishers, 1990).

2. *Heirs Together of Life,* by Charles and Norma Ellis (Banner of Truth Books, P.O. Box 621 Carlisle, PA 17013).

3. *Marriage Savers* by Michael McManus (Zondervan, 1993), chapter 7.

4. *Restoring a Loving Marriage,* by Jay Kesler with Joe Musser (David C. Cook, 1989).

5. *Husband and Wives: The Best of Friends* by Otis and Deigie Andrews (LifeWay Press, 1994).

---

[1]Jay Kesler, *Restoring a Loving Marriage* (Elgin: David C. Cook, 1989), 138.

Take Into Account Male and Female Differences

Many male-female conflicts are based on profound gender differences. Understanding them is an answer.

Ed, from New Jersey, had been in a troubled marriage for 31 years and had gone through marriage and family counseling to no avail. He came across the book, *Men Are From Mars, Women are From Venus* by John Gray[1], and wrote me: "I learned more in the first two dozen pages than from all of the counseling over the past thirty years."

Gray says men and women differ in all areas. They think and communicate differently; they feel, respond, love, and need differently. Someone who did not know better might even think that men and women were from entirely different planets.

So what happens is that men and women end up with all kinds of relationship problems by not understanding these differences.

MEN: HOW TO UNDERSTAND WOMEN

Women talk about problems to *feel better*. They're not really looking for solutions. Men, on the other hand, assume that if a woman is describing problems, she *wants an answer*.

In a class for engaged couples, Harriet and I role-played a situation from Gray's book of a wife coming home exhausted after work.

Harriet (home after an exhausting day): "There's so much to do; I've no time for myself."

Mike: "You should quit that job—it's too hard."

Harriet: "But I like my job. They just want me to change."

Mike: "Don't listen to them. Just do what you can."

Harriet: "I forgot to call my aunt today."

Mike: "Don't worry. She'll understand."

Harriet: "With what she's going through? She needs me."

Mike: "You worry too much. That's why you're unhappy."

Harriet: "I am not unhappy. Why can't you just *listen* to me?

Mike: "I *am* listening."

Harriet: "Oh, why do I even bother?"

Thus, my "solutions" only made things worse. Women don't offer solutions when someone else is talking. They listen patiently, with empathy. Not until I had been married ten years did I learn my wife only wanted me to listen. Now when Harriet comes home, it's like this:

Harriet: "There's so much to do, I have no time for me."

Mike: "Sounds like you had a bad day."

Harriet: "They expect me to change everything overnight."

Mike (After a pause): "Hmmm."

Harriet: "I even forgot to call my aunt."

Mike: "Oh, really?"

Harriet: "She needs me so much right now. I feel so bad."

Mike (Gives her a hug): "You're such a loving person!"

Harriet: "I love talking with you. You make me feel good."

Women also "score" gifts differently than men do. Each gift to her has equal value. A poem means as much as a new dress. So, men—here's some advice. **Devote more time to little things.** In returning home, give her a hug. Then ask specific questions about her day. Give her 20 minutes of your undivided attention—turn off the TV, wait to read the mail, and don't pick up the newspaper. Praise her looks. Surprise her with a love note.

WOMEN: HOW TO UNDERSTAND MEN

When your husband boasts to you about completing a big project, which he thinks is a big deal, don't treat it lightly.

If you want something, be direct and brief: "Would you please take out the trash?" He will respond. If he makes a mistake, don't say, "I told you so."

Another book on gender differences is *You Just Don't Understand* by Deborah Tannen. She says that boys and girls grow up in different cultures.

Boys play outside, in large groups that are hierarchically structured. Their groups have a leader who tells others what to do and resists what others propose. . . . Boys say, "Gimme that!" and "Get outta here!"

Girls play in small groups or in pairs; the center of a girl's life is a best friend. . . . In their games, such as jump rope or hopscotch, everyone gets a turn. Many of their activities (such as playing house) do not have winners and losers. They say, "Let's do this," and "How about doing that?" Girls are not accustomed to jockeying for status in an obvious way; they are more concerned that they be liked.[2]

If a man and woman are driving and she says, "Would you like to stop for a Coke?" he's likely to think about it, decide he'd rather get to their destination instead of stopping. So he'll answer honestly and say, "No."

But his wife's feelings will be hurt. He didn't realize she was not asking a simple factual question. Rather, she was opening negotiations on what they'll do next. But it went right over his head.

In short, **men and women are different**. Understanding differences can help us as marriage savers, both with our own marriages as well as when we guide others.

Biblical References

Genesis 1:27; Matthew 19:6; Galatians 5:25-26; Philippians 2:3;

Other Resources

1. *Men Are From Mars, Women Are From Venus* by John Gray (HarperCollins, 1992).

2. *You Just Don't Understand* by Deborah Tannen (Ballantine Books, 1990).

---

[1]John Gray, *Men Are from Mars, Women Are from Venus* (New York: HarperCollins, 1992), 5-19.

[2]Deborah Tannen, *You Just Don't Understand* (New York: Ballantine Books, 1990), 43-44.

Make the Lord a Third Partner in Your Marriage

A study of 600 couples with long and successful marriages reveals their secret: **a Christ-centered home.**

That study by Dr. James Dobson was amplified in his book, *Love For a Lifetime.* He reported that a couple who prays together and depends on the Bible "for solutions to the stresses of living has a distinct advantage over the family with no faith. . . . Marriage and parenthood were **His** ideas, and He tells us in His Word how to live together in peace and harmony. Everything from handling money to sexual attitudes is discussed in Scripture."[1]

The purpose of marriage is not simply to draw two people together to carry on the human race. Rather, it's designed for us to more fully realize our natures. As two people become one in love and intimacy, their purpose is to also draw closer to God.

In marriage, two people execute a covenant to love and care for one another in mutual trust and faithfulness. You promise to love, honor, and care for each other in all circumstances so long as you both shall live. This is the kind of relationship God wants with us no matter what our marital status.

God will not abandon you (see Josh. 1:5); He will

always be with you, in all kinds of adversity (see Ps. 46:1). And this relationship is meant to last.

In your marriage it is not enough to simply make room for God; without Him as central to your marriage, the relationship is *incomplete*.

Christian marriage is often pictured as a triangle: man and woman at the base, with God at the apex. As the couple moves closer to God, they move closer to each other. God created the concept of marriage and He helps to make it work.

God planned it so He could be an integral part of the marriage process of growing, learning, and loving. Yet, He must be invited to participate.

Couples need interaction, not just with each other but also with God. The couple already knows that if they are in agreement, their oneness helps them. When they ask God to be a part of their union, the marriage relationship is *fully complete* and can withstand the stresses and adversity that pull at their marriage.

"A cord of three strands is not quickly broken," wrote Solomon in Ecclesiastes 4:12. If you invite the Lord to join your marriage, it will endure.

The Lord Can Become Your Partner

Each morning Harriet and I have a quiet time together before starting our day. We enjoy coffee as we chat. I may read a chapter of Scripture or a devotional page. We pray for each other, our children, and our day ahead.

Proverbs is my favorite book of the Bible. It's packed with wisdom, giving us the mind of God on how to live. There are 31 chapters of Proverbs, exactly enough for a month. Each chapter is full of insight, and since there's no plot line, if I skip a day, it doesn't matter.

There are countless devotional books and tapes to help you focus daily upon God. *Heirs Together of Life* is one such book. Charles and Norma Ellis suggest the man do the devotional reading, followed by a sharing of mutual thoughts and reactions, closing with each person praying.

Quiet Times for Couples is another popular daily devotional.H. Norman Wright combines his experience as a psychologist and counselor with the spiritual insights of a biblical scholar, and the authoritative writing of a journalist.

Wright notes that we live in a "hurry up and get there" society which does not welcome waiting upon the Lord (Isa. 40:31). He says there are times when it is best to say to one another, "Let's pray about this and wait upon God for an answer." Have you tried that recently?

That's exactly how Harriet and I treat our toughest decisions. And that's the process which makes the Lord a third partner of our marriage. We once had a difficult choice to make about whether to move from Connecticut to Maryland. So we took the matter to the Lord in prayer and daily discussion. We left the results to Him. We decided to move, and everything worked out just as He promised it would (see Rom. 8:28).

There is no end to the satisfaction, joy, and sense of completeness a couple can have when they **make God a partner** in their marriage.

Biblical References
Job 11:18-19; Proverbs 1:33; 3:24; Isaiah 40:31; Jeremiah 29:12; John 15:5, 7; James 5:16

Other Resources
1. An abundance of devotional materials for couples can be found at your Christian bookstore.

2. *Restoring a Loving Marriage* (David C. Cook, 1989), chapters 9 and 10.

---

[1]Dobson, *Love for a Lifetime*, 53-54.

Experience an Enrichment Weekend to Revive and Strengthen Your Marriage

Virtually every marriage can be made better by attending a structured marriage enrichment retreat. Good marriages can become great ones!

Harriet and I had a good marriage, but in 1976 it was once under great stress. My work in Connecticut was over and I'd gotten a job in Washington. I'd board a train in Stamford at 2 a.m. Mondays, roll into Washington, work all week, and come home exhausted Friday night, arriving at 11 p.m.

Harriet tolerated this schedule graciously for months, even preparing a lovely late dinner Fridays. On Saturdays and Sundays I was buried in writing. I was *not* a good father or husband. During those months, friends at church began suggesting, "Why don't you and Harriet go on a Marriage Encounter weekend?"

I asked, "What is it?" They were mysterious. "It's a way to strengthen your marriage."

Miffed, I retorted, "I *have* a good marriage."

"But Marriage Encounter is designed to make a good marriage better!" As I thought about it, it seemed like a good idea, but when I mentioned it to Harriet, she said, "No!" rather sharply. "Besides, we can't afford it," Harriet added. So I repeated that excuse the next time someone suggested our going. "But your way is already paid for. Go, and we'll even baby-sit your kids."

Harriet was now out of excuses, so we drove 80 miles to a motel, arriving for dinner on Friday. Our first surprise was that every couple who had urged us to go was already there! They had decorated the place with balloons and presented us a basket of fruit.

After dinner, three couples made the first of many intimate presentations, drawing from the experience of their own marriages.

We then returned to our motel room assigned to write the first of many "love letters"—describing what we liked about our spouse and our marriage. Then we exchanged the letters and discussed them privately.

TV sets were unplugged, and we put away all watches to totally focus on each other. Suddenly I was glad I was there spending time alone with Harriet.

The talks from the leader couples were often deeply moving. Father Bob, an Episcopal priest, confessed, "I was married to my job." (I winced, for that sounded exactly like me!) He continued, "I gave little time to Susan. The parish was my world."

When Susan spoke, she was weeping, "A conspiracy kept me from my husband. It is as if he were born with a two-way radio, responding to everyone but his wife. I was ignored."

Later, we were asked to write a "love letter" to our spouse concerning something "that I couldn't or didn't share." I was shocked by Harriet's letter. She wrote that she felt bruised by my work in Washington. "You left me for a year and a half quite voluntarily. I felt deserted." Then, when we discussed the letters, she added, "This is NO marriage. I never see you during the week—you work all the time and don't even spend time with the boys. This isn't why I married you. You're a workaholic. You love your work, not me."

I broke down and cried. I was so absorbed in the difficulties of my life and work that I hadn't realized its impact on Harriet. I asked her for forgiveness. I didn't know she'd held such deep, burning anger within her all those months.

That experience taught me that our Marriage Encounter leaders were right, **it's essential to take time out with your spouse every day**.

Harriet and I fell back in love that weekend. Our experience is not rare. Some 30 studies report that 80 to 90 percent of the 1.5 million Marriage Encounter attendees found a new joy in their marriage.

There are other effective weekend retreats also designed to refresh a marriage. Some 16,000 attend Festivals of Marriage each year. The theme changes each year, always focusing on a specific issue. Sixty percent of attendees return each year.

Marriage Enrichment is a weekend retreat started by David and Vera Mace. These events are attended by some 18,000 couples each year.

A Weekend to Remember is another such event, attended by over 22,000 couples each year. It is part of the Family Life Ministries of Campus Crusade For Christ.

These marriage renewal and retreat weekends are so intense and meaningful that they are often life-changing.

Larry Lewis, President of the Home Mission Board of the Southern Baptist Convention, attended a Protestant version of Marriage Encounter and said "We naively believed we had no need for any such experience since our marriage was so happy.

However, very few, if any, weekends before or since, have been more blessed and meaningful."

Dr. James Dobson confesses that he attended "for professional reasons, not expecting to get anything relevant to my wife and me. If there is anything I felt that Shirley and I didn't need, it was help in communicating. I have rarely been more wrong. Marriage Encounter gave Shirley and me the deepest, most intimate exchange of feelings we had known in 20 years. . . . It proved to be one of the highlights of my life."

Talk to anyone who has attended a weekend marriage retreat, and you will be given a similar response. You owe it to your own marriage to schedule such an event. You might consider paying another couple's way as a gift to their marriage. Either way, it's an investment that will pay on-going dividends.

Biblical References
Psalm 32:8; Isaiah 46:11; Acts 20:35; 1 Timothy 6:6; Hebrews 12:1-2

Other Resources
1. **Marriage Encounter**, call 1-800-795-LOVE or write: Worldwide Marriage Encounter, 1908 E. Highland, #A, San Bernardino, CA 92404.

2. **Marriage Enrichment**, call 1-800-634-8325 or write P.O. Box 10596, Winston-Salem, NC 27108.

3. **A Weekend to Remember**, call 1-501-223-8663 or write: Family Life Ministries, P.O. Box 23840, Little Rock, AR 72221.

4. **Festival of Marriage**, call 1-615-251-2277 or write: Festival of Marriage, 127 Ninth Ave. North, Nashville, TN 37234.

5. *Marriage Savers* by Michael McManus (Zondervan, 1993), chapter 9.

6. *Marriage Savers Resource Collection*, video program 4.

Try These 17 Steps for Deeply Troubled Marriages

Couples whose own marriages once nearly failed are uniquely qualified to help marriages in trouble. In 1987 Father Dick McGinnis of St. David's Episcopal Church in Jacksonville, Florida, made an announcement to his congregation, "I want to meet after the service with people whose marriages have been on the rocks, but who have successfully come off of them—people who have been in extreme difficulty and have threatened divorce, but who are in recovery."

To his surprise ten couples showed up. He confessed to them, "I have more marriage counseling than I can handle. There is no way to keep up with it. I prayed about it. What came to me was I was not to look at the problem, but at the solution."

He recalled how Alcoholics Anonymous got started, with "Bill" and "Dr. Bob" helping each other stay sober. So they began helping other alcoholics. AA then developed the "12 Steps" that have helped millions stay sober.

Father McGinnis met with seven of those ten couples over time to see if there was a common thread for marriages to be restored. The couples shared openly and deeply. Father McGinnis asked each, "What did you do to restore your marriage?"

At first their stories seemed radically different. However, there was much in common. Six of the seven had been to Marriage Encounter. More important, each went through certain similar spiritual steps that enabled them to rebuild their marriages.

Marriage Ministry

After months of review, the couples worked out what ultimately became *17 Marriage Ministry Action Statements*.

For example, each made a "commitment to follow Jesus as my Savior and Lord," as one story illustrates. Lowell said, "We had tried humanistic books like *I'm OK. You're OK.* None of it was working. So we said, 'Why not try God? What else have we got to lose?' We went to St. David's. We became 'born again' We realized the Lord really loved us and we began to love ourselves." Accepting Christ was the starting point to their restored marriage.

Franki, Lowell's wife, added, "I realized that the problem was with *myself.* I needed to change." She explained, "I was head of the house in everything and he just followed. He did football and the garbage. He left his laundry on the floor. He did not help discipline the kids." Then she saw part of the problem was her sharp tongue. She'd been nagging constantly before she made a commitment to Christ. When she changed, Lowell noticed immediately. "She stopped complaining!" So he was motivated to pick up his clothes—which was a kind act that she noticed and caused her to be more affectionate that night. He even decided to assume the responsibility to discipline the kids.

Franki learned *she could not change her mate. But with God's help she could change.* And remarkably, *her change prompted him to change.* What was before a downward spiral reversed itself.

As the seven couples shared their stories, their own marriages improved. Those seven couples have now worked with 40 other couples whose marriages were deeply troubled, and there's been only one separation! That's a 98 percent success rate!

In Ephesians 4:12, the Apostle Paul says the job of a pastor is "to prepare God's people for works of service." What greater need is there in every church than saving marriages?

Over half of America's marriages fail. Father McGinnis reflects, "I started this looking to see if God had a way for marriages to be restored. He does. It's summed up in the 17 Marriage Ministry Steps. Any pastor could use them to equip recovering couples to help others. The couples' personal experience breathes life into the steps."

MARRIAGE MINISTRY 17 STEPS

1. Through other Christians, find hope for our marriage.

2. Personally experience God's love and forgiveness.

3. Make a personal decision/commitment to love: Christ, mate, self.

4. Make a decision/commitment to follow Christ as Savior and Lord.

5. Once obedient to God, begin to love by His standards, not ours.

6. Become accountable to God for my behavior, thoughts, and actions, and become aware of accountability to others.

7. Make a decision to stay together.

8. Make a decision to forgive my mate and myself.

9. Accept my mate as he/she is.

10. Realize that the problem was with myself.

11. Begin to look at myself as needing to change to be able to love, no matter what. Become aware that I need to change, become willing to change, learn

what and how to change; begin change with God's help.

12. Make an examination of my role in marriage according to God's Word and change accordingly with God's help.

13. Accept change in my mate.

14. Through Christ, begin trusting enough to increasingly put whole self in the care of my mate.

15. Learn to communicate honestly and openly in love.

16. Learn to put God and mate ahead of self (humble before the Lord).

17. Realize we are still in process, that we must share what we have found with others.

Biblical References

Ephesians 4:12; 5:21-33; Philippians 2:1-4; 1 Corinthians 13:4-6

Other Resources

1. *Marriage Savers* by Michael McManus (Zondervan, 1993), chapter 10.

2. *Marriage Savers Resource Collection,* video program 5.

3. See the *Marriage Savers Leader's Study Guide* for help on how to start such a ministry in your church.

A N S W E R   19

Consider Retrouvaille for Deeply Troubled Marriages

Divorce is devastating. Divorce affects the couple involved, their extended families, and children they may have. Divorce creates a series of events that brings chaos into many lives. Divorce can be avoided. *Even deeply troubled marriages can be restored to health.* The most dramatic and successful initiative to pull marriages from divorce courts was created in Quebec by Catholic lay leaders of Marriage Encounter who observed that the weekend retreat was not reaching many of those couples already headed toward divorce.

They designed a new weekend, followed by six additional sessions, led by mentor couples whose *own* marriages had once nearly dissolved. Called "Retrouvaille" (French for "Rediscovery", pronounced ret-roo-vie), the movement is now in 100 metropolitan areas of the United States.

Its results are spectacular. In Fort Worth, Texas, 40 percent of 817 couples attending *were already separated.* Yet, *70 percent have rebuilt their marriages!* In Buffalo, New York, the success rate was 93 percent.

Retrouvaille attendees must agree in advance that

*they want to make their marriage work. And, if a
third party is involved, that outside affair or relationship must end.*

Leader couples share with attendees how they
nearly destroyed their own marriages. One man,
Bob Pate, confessed his affairs. But Marie, his wife,
admitted "I never faced *my responsibility* for his unfaithfulness."

Leaders explain, "Love is a decision, not a feeling. Feelings come and go. Love as a decision gives
us control over ourselves."

After each lecture, attendees return to their rooms
with an assignment to write out their feelings.
Afterwards, they exchange notebooks, read, and
talk privately.

They repeat this intensive process over a weekend, and lay a foundation for healing. Then they
meet at least six more times with other "graduates."

Two of those who heard Bob and Marie share
their story were Mike and Brenda. A traveling computer expert, Mike had frequented bars and picked
up women for brief affairs.

He got away with it for years until he had a fling
with a woman whose husband found out and con-
fronted him as did Mike's wife, Brenda. Shocked
and angry, she said, "I wanted to kill. If I would
have had a gun in my hand, he would not be alive.
It was horrible." Their screaming confrontation took
place in front of their boys, ages nine and six. The
frightened, tearful children had never even seen
them argue before!

How did Retrouvaille help? Brenda and Mike saw
other couples who—like them—had been through
much misery in their lives. They heard firsthand
how they'd come through it. Hearing such success
stories is *genuinely motivating*. It makes couples
want the same happiness in their marriage.

Retrouvaille leads to healed marriages by using
other couples who have overcome troubled mar-

riages. This effective process equips these couples with communication tools and the loving heart to continue to work on their marriages. And the process cycle begins again with other couples.

Four years after Brenda and Mike's experience with Retrouvaille, their teenage son, Jason, wrote them an anniversary letter: "Thank you for being mine and Jacob's parents, and all you do for me. You stayed together mostly because you did not want to lose us or hurt us, and we respect you for making that decision."

Biblical References
Psalm 42:11; 71:20; Isaiah 55:7; Ephesians 5:21-33; 1 John 1:7-9; 3:20

Other Resources
1. For information about **Retrouvaille,** call Roger and Pat Bate (713) 455-1656.

2. *Marriage Savers* by Michael McManus (Zondervan, 1993), chapter 10.

3. *Marriage Savers Resource Collection,* video program 5.

Insuring Marriage

*Consider Reconciliation
If You Are Separated or
Divorced*

Even when a marriage is torn asunder, it is possible—and important—to achieve a level of reconciliation. Are you divorced, separated, or likely to be one of 1.2 million couples who split apart this year? If you are not, no doubt you know a couple that will join those ranks. There is hope. One answer is reconciliation.

Mention the word **"reconciliation"** to an angry, separated spouse, and the likely response is "No way! I don't want to have anything to do with him/her." Even so, Dr. Jim Talley suggests, "It's *never* too late!" He should know. He's worked with 13,000 "singles" over the past 25 years, many of whom were once married.

The normal assumption is that it is unlikely or impossible to achieve reconciliation. Talley observes that, "The model American marital advice of pastors and friends comes in five words: 'Get on with your life.' In other words, forget your spouse. Find someone else."

Problems aren't solved by divorcing and remarrying. Second marriages have a 60 percent divorce rate. Why? "You tend to drag all the difficulties of the first marriage into the second," observes Talley. "The tendency is to choose the same character deficiencies in the second partner as the first. I have seen people marry three alcoholics in a row."

Fortunately, "Reconciliation Instruction" has helped hundreds of couples restore harmony, love, and marriage to once hopeless relationships.

More than half of those who are separated and take the course are able to save their marriages. And even most others who do divorce are able to restore a sense of civility to their relationships.

The prime time to offer Reconciliation Instruction is immediately after the separation, and before either person has begun dating again. In fact, a prerequisite to taking the four-month reconciliation course is an agreement by both people not to date anyone else.

There are other prerequisites:

1. No changes are to be made in the legal status of the relationship. If you are living separately, continue to do so.

2. Do not talk or even think about remarriage during the four months, to protect the relationship from unrealistic expectations.

3. Limit the physical relationship to the lowest level desired by either partner.

The course also can be taken by divorced couples. However, Talley warns, "Reconciliation does not necessarily mean remarriage. At first it may only mean reducing the danger level when children are exchanged for visits," (when some couples have their most violent arguments).

The primary goal is to enable those who are angry, bitter, and hostile to be friendly again. It's possible to bring back harmony, whether separated, divorced, or remarried.

The course requires reading *Reconcilable Differences,* writing in a workbook, and meeting with your partner eight times to read and discuss what each has written. Finally, they must attend eight sessions with an instructor or mentor couple.

Mary heard about the course in church. Immature and only 19 when she married Bob, she was very submissive, which he, a corporate climber, enjoyed. But as three children came along, she changed. Mary became assertive, which Bob didn't like, so he buried himself in a 12 to 15 hour work day. "I felt completely out of his life, and perceived there must be another woman," Mary says.

Bob recalls, "I was a workaholic, no husband at all, a money-maker. Communication stopped. What caused separation was my temper got out of hand. There was no physical abuse, but only because I restrained myself."

Mary told him to leave and he did, but continued paying the bills.

She was bitter, depressed, and felt utterly hopeless when she began Reconciliation Instruction. Her feelings were natural. Mary invited Bob to the course. At first, he declined, but later said, "What hit home with me was she found a peace in what we were going through, and I was on a roller coaster."

Mary's one-sided change made her very attractive to Bob. So he attended and asked to move back in. Mary and her counselor said no, that Bob had to take four months of Reconciliation Instruction first.

Bob was furious. "I want to move in with my wife, and then take the course."

The counselor explained, "The success rate is dramatically improved if you remain apart."

Bob reluctantly agreed. Then "lights turned on" for him; he got his spiritual life together. The most important lesson from the course was learning the skills of how to resolve conflict. Bob and Mary are now back together in a growing marriage.

What should you do when your spouse won't take the course? "First," says Talley, "Stabilize your life spiritually, emotionally, lovingly, and financially. Second, sit still and wait. Do not date, so that when the other person cycles back (and most do) you are a more mature, stable person and available to respond." Talley says that the other person is enticed to come back by the fragrance of your changed life.

Changed people are able to change people.

Biblical References

James 1:19-20; Psalm 37:8; Ephesians 4:31-32; Colossians 3:8; Proverbs 16:7; Hebrews 13:6

Other Resources

1. *Reconcilable Differences* by Jim Talley, (Thomas Nelson Publishers, 1991)

2. *Reconciliation Instruction Workbooks,* published by Jim Talley, available by calling (405) 789-2900.

3. *How to Reconcile a Marriage,* one-hour audio tape from Focus on the Family, with Dr. James Dobson, Jim Talley and two couples whose marriages he helped restore. Write Focus on the Family, Colorado Springs, CO 80995.

4. *Marriage Savers Resource Collection,* video program 6.

5. *Divorce Recovery* by Harold Ivan Smith (Broadman & Holman, 1994).

Insuring Marriage

Stepfamily Support Groups Provide Mutual Help and Encouragement

United Methodist Singles Pastor Dick Dunn of the Atlanta area didn't pay much attention to Joe and Carla Martin when they asked him for help with their tumultuous stepparent family. After all, the couple was from the church—surely there would be no real problems in their second marriage. Or so he thought.

However, Dick recalled the explosion that occurred after his own divorce when his daughter, Kim, came home from college one Christmas. Dick and his second wife Betty, had just moved to the Atlanta area. When his daughter arrived for the holidays, Dick took several days showing Kim all the sights. But Betty felt like a fifth wheel.

Betty labored over the Christmas turkey, but when she was ready to serve it, Kim was listening to rock music. "Would you please put on Christmas carols?" Betty asked.

Not only was Kim's answer "No," but Dick sided with her. "Why not let her play her music?"

The next day, Dick said to Betty, "Kim and I want to eat Chinese. Do you want to go with us?"

Betty retorted, "No. And I won't be here when you get back. I'm going back home to Ohio."

That got Dick's attention. Like many divorced fathers who see their kids occasionally, Dick didn't see the problem with his daughter's behavior and didn't realize he was neglecting his wife whenever Kim was around.

Dick resolved his immediate crisis, then remembered the Martin's plea for help. He created a "Stepfamily Support Group." The group has helped more than 200 couples discover that they aren't alone in facing severe conflict.

Joe and Carla shared their story at the group's first meeting—how they'd expected "bliss and a new family" not "constant fighting and bickering." "It was the most painful experience I have ever been through. I set deadlines. If it's not better in six months, I'll not put up with it any longer," Carla said. "When his kids visited on weekends, Joe didn't discipline them since he only saw them a few days a week." His son Brian now admits that he did things "to purposely drive Carla crazy." Joe recalls, "I never wanted to believe anything bad about my kids."

Sally and Van Malone remember the shock of their first Christmas. Each had both a boy and girl from a previous marriage, and the four kids seemed to get along well before the wedding. Their vision was a "Brady Bunch" family.

But that first Christmas was a horror. They discovered that three different mini-family traditions and three separate timetables had to be negotiated: Van and his kids; Sally and hers; Sally's ex-husband and his new wife who lived nearby. Conflicts between the three families were fierce.

Van was a widower whose first wife died of cancer. His daughter Rachel assumed the leadership role of her mother and ran their household for five years—during the two years her mother was sick and died, and afterward, when her father was a single parent.

Rachel was unwilling to give her father up to this new woman. Right after the honeymoon, she announced, "I don't want another mother." When Sally went to take a shower, Rachel would take *her* shower, draining the hot water. "She treated me like a piece of furniture, talking only to Van, never to me," said Sally.

Rachel accused her dad, "You never really loved my mother." She reasoned, "If Dad loves Sally, he never loved Mom."

Fortunately, Roswell's Stepfamily Support Group had already been organized when Sally and Van married. After a few months of marriage they shared with the support group their experience of conflict with Rachel and the other kids and Sally's ex-husband.

"It sounds *normal* to us," a chorus replied.

That was a great relief to hear," Sally recalls. People think what they are experiencing is unique to them. In stepfamilies the finger of blame gets pointed at everyone—with no one realizing that stepparent-stepchild-biological parent conflict is normal.

Roswell's stepfamily group has now worked with 200 couples in turmoil, only 10 of whom got divorced. That's only a *5 percent divorce* rate for those in second marriages compared to a normal 60 percent!

"It saved our marriage," many say. How? Dick Dunn outlines lessons in *Willing To Try Again: Steps Toward Blending a Family.*

1. Changing rules: Single parent households tend to be lax on rules and kids help shape them. Blended families return to rules imposed by parents, sparking explosions. Go slowly in changing rules.

2. Time with parent: Single parents who once

spent hours with children tend to spend no time with them after the marriage. That is unwise.

3. The "wicked" stepparent: The biological parent must elevate the importance of the stepparent. If kids ask a father permission to do something, he can say, "Let me check with Sue." That involves his partner. Later he can say, "Sue thinks it makes sense," creating goodwill in the mind of the child because of the stepparent's approval.

4. Family conferences: Stepfamilies often meet weekly, giving each person a chance to say anything, respectful or not. "I don't like you," a stepson might say.

Sue might respond, "But we live together. Let's work things out in a way we can both accept."

5. Couple time alone: Couples must continue to have "dates" and weekend getaways without kids, to nurture their own relationship.

6. Create stepfamily groups: Every church should form a stepfamily support group.

Couples who have remarried and who have the problems of stepchildren, ex-spouses, and the clashes of stepfamilies need to take steps to deal with these problem areas. *Nothing could do more to save second marriages from second divorces.*

Biblical References
Psalm 121:7-8; 1 Corinthians 10:13; Hebrews 10:35-36; 12:14; James 1:3-6; 1 Peter 3:13; 1 John 4:11

Other Resources
1. Contact the Stepfamily Association of America for help organizing a support group (402) 477-STEP.

2. *Marriage Savers Resource Collection,* video program 6, features Rev. Dick Dunn's Stepfamily Support Group.

3. *Willing To Try Again: Steps Toward Blending a Family* by Dick Dunn (Judson Press, 1993).

A N S W E R 2 2

Insuring Marriage

Single Adults — Insuring Their Future Marriages and Being Marriage Savers

Single adult Christians should help transform their church into a place that helps them develop and provide programs and activities for building up other single adults and couples while helping to create lifelong marriages.

Many adults in most churches are single, but few are in church leadership, maybe because their priority is in finding a lifelong mate. But those singles fail to realize that *the church could be their best ally* in that task, especially when their leadership service consists of helping other single adults (never marrieds and formerly marrieds) find answers to their questions about marriage.

Being single is as valid a biblical model for Christian service as being married. Jesus, Paul, and Martha were unmarried. But since many church single adults want to marry, they need to be involved in understanding the marriage relationship.

QUESTIONS FOR A SINGLE ADULT GATHERING

Why not have your next single adult retreat or seminar focus on tough marital questions? Some could be based on the Answers reported in this book.

1. What can help single adults avoid a bad marriage?

Chastity increases the odds of a lifelong marriage by two-thirds. Are you committed to not "live together"? How can you build a good marriage, or understand what's wrong with divorce?

Help your church promote an abstinence campaign in which teenagers and single adults promise God that they will be sexually pure. How can your church also offer help to seriously dating couples? Ask for a similar pledge of chastity so they can build a relationship on God. Relationship Instruction includes such a pledge.

Does your church offer PREPARE, the premarital inventory that can predict whether a marriage will end in divorce? The best time to take it is when a seriously dating couple is trying to decide whether to marry.

Single adults can provide real leadership in this area, but may even benefit from it as well, since PREPARE's creators say the best time to take this inventory is when the singles who make up the couple have not yet decided to marry.

2. How can our church insure future marriages?

See to it that your church offers its seriously dating singles some kind of Relationship Instruction. While half who take it do not marry, of those who do, more than 90 percent have a lasting marriage. *That's real "Marriage Insurance!"*

Is your church's premarital program rigorous? Is it mandatory? Are mature married mentor couples involved? Are there lectures and classes for dating singles on tough marital issues: managing money, sex in marriage, conflict resolution, communication? Are engaged couples taught biblical principles?

Is there a minimum time for marriage preparation? Does your church encourage engaged couples to attend a retreat? If your church offers these proven steps to single adults who become engaged, their odds of a lifelong marriage increase dramatically.

Of course, none of these steps will help you, as a single adult, to find the right person! At least not directly. But if your church is known as a place that cherishes single adults so much that it takes serious steps to help unmarried people build a lifelong marriage, your congregation will attract a larger number of single adults and people who are, like you, deeply committed to spiritual values. And from this company of singles, many may meet a life partner.

3. Does our church have a special focus on those who are "single again"—separated or divorced?

Those who are "single again" after a separation or divorce have special needs that are different from single adults who have never been married. For example, a recently separated person should not be encouraged to date. Retrouvaille and Reconciliation Instruction are programs that can save more than half of separated marriages, and even reunite some of the already divorced couples. Separated persons are still married and churches should use these programs to provide possible rebonding by separated husbands and wives.

Finally, you can offer divorced single adults "divorce recovery" classes that can help a new single-again person rebuild the self-esteem that's inevitably shattered by separation and divorce.

Biblical References
Proverbs 2:5-7; Ecclesiastes 2:26; Matthew 16:24; Hebrews 11:6; James 1:12

Other Resources

1. *Christian Single* magazine (product # 1806). Order by calling 1-800-458-2772 or write Customer Service Center; 127 Ninth Avenue, North; Nashville, TN 37234.

2. *A Time for Healing: Coming to Terms with Your Divorce* by Harold Ivan Smith (LifeWay Press, 1994).

3. *Willing To Try Again* by Dick Dunn (Judson Press, 1993).

4. *Marriage Savers Resource Collection,* video program 6.

5. Focus on the Family single parents' magazine. Call (719) 531-5181.

6. To receive a packet on organizing a single adult ministry, contact: Single Adult Ministry; (MSN 151); 127 Ninth Avenue, North; Nashville, TN 37234.

7. *Singles Adult Ministries Journal,* P.O. Box 62056, Colorado Springs, CO 80962-2056.

A N S W E R   2 3

Insuring Marriage

Participating in Church Can Help Save a Marriage

Pollsters have said that people who participate in church on a regular basis have better results in social and personal relationships. The strength that comes from being actively involved in a church family has been well documented.

People who attend church tend to live longer, happier, and more productive lives. They have inner strength that helps them cope with life's stresses. There is a common unity and single focus of faith that brings men and women together. For thousands of years, churches have provided purpose and common values.

Because of strong moral and ethical values among those who are church members, single adults who are seeking a mate are more likely to be satisfied with the choices they find at church.

Church has become a place of refuge, a home for us to commune with "brothers and sisters" who are like-minded.

While not perfect, our churches still offer more hope than any other institution to those who face unusual problems and difficulties in life or society. That's why those who are looking for a marriage partner or facing marital difficulties should be attending church.

The spiritual strength that is obtained from an attachment to a church can make a difference in how well a person does in selecting a mate or how well marriage difficulties can be resolved. Church fellowship, prayer, and pastoral counsel are not usually available outside the church. The vital sources of emotional and spiritual strength found in a church can make a significant difference for those who are in the throes of divorce.

Yet, we know that the divorce rate among church members is nearly the same as society in general. And not all pastors and their congregations are well equipped to help their members deal with divorce.

Even strong churches with a myriad of ministries often do nothing to strengthen existing marriages or save troubled ones. Indeed, some even separate married couples. My church has a men's retreat and a women's retreat, but only newlyweds have couples' retreats. Harriet and I are working to organize a Marriage Encounter weekend for all interested married couples.

The initiative has to come from couples like you and Harriet and me, with a heart for strengthening marriage. What does your church do to help newlyweds succeed? Half of the newly wed are horrified by the conflicts they are experiencing. Is there a **mentoring program** available for them?

Are **marriage classes** offered to small groups—even three or four couples—for an objective view of their strengths and areas for needed growth. Is there a **Bible Study** for newlyweds?

Has every married couple been urged to attend Marriage Encounter, Marriage Enrichment, or a Festival of Marriage **weekend retreat** to make their marriage better? If not, why not? Why don't you go?

If your experience is powerful, you'll be an effective advocate for church-wide change.

Many churches are helping singles and couples get help for **marriage preparation** or **counseling**. An Assembly of God church in Illinois puts $5,000 into its budget to pay for a Valentine's weekend for every couple. Should this be a part of your church's budget? If marriage is the bedrock institution of our society, it deserves support in both money and time.

Our church recruits couples with 20-50 years of successful marital experience to **mentor younger couples**. Harriet and I have trained 22 other couples who are investing themselves in the lives of seriously dating couples, engaged, and newlyweds. It is a joyous ministry, and one that deepens the marriages of those of us who are mentors as much as those we mentor.

Many churches offer **courses to strengthen marriage**, such as the *Covenant Marriage* courses of the Sunday School Board. Those also provide great training for mentors.

Other churches have developed **plans to intervene** with couples on the verge of divorce and save some of the most deeply troubled marriages. Father Dick McGinnis, an Episcopal minister in Florida, created a support group similar to Alcoholics Anonymous that is designed to rescue and heal marriages. His story was told in Answer 18.

Other church leaders can offer this ministry for an effective reduction in the divorce rate in their churches. Or they can develop their own principles. Ask couples who have survived bad marriages if they would help couples currently in trouble.

Father McGinnis' 7 couples have worked with 40 troubled marriages in Jacksonville since 1987 and none have divorced, though one did separate. Your church can have such a healing ministry that can save seemingly hopeless marriages.

Retrouvaille is a **weekend retreat for couples with marital problems** that brings hope and healing to still other couples (see Answer 19).

Even if divorce has already occurred, your church can minister to you. Many churches have established **divorce recovery workshops** and **support groups**, providing a loving, Christian community for healing.

There are **support groups for helping second marriages**, such as the Stepfamily Support Group established by Roswell United Methodist Church in Georgia.

For a long time, churches ignored the need to help young people choose the right marriage partner, prepare them with instruction, and address the problems of troubled marriages. These churches simply refused to acknowledge that Christians were divorcing in about the same numbers as the rest of society. But now, more than ever, **the church is the place to go for encouragement, support, and spiritual reinforcement.** Churches can and should be marriage savers.

Biblical References

2 Chronicles 15:2; Isaiah 58:9; Acts 17:27; Colossians 3:12-13; Titus 2:1-5; Hebrews 11:6

Other Resources

1. *Finding A Church You Can Call Home: a Complete Guide to Making One of the Most Important Decisions of Your Life* by George Barna, (Regal Books, 1992).

2. *Marriage Savers Resource Collection,* video program 1.

3. *Marriage Savers* by Michael McManus (Zondervan, 1993), chapters 7 and 10.

4. *Covenant Marriage: Partnership and Commitment* by Diana Garland and Betty Hassler (LifeWay Press, 1989).

5. *Communication and Intimacy: Covenant Marriage* by Gary Chapman and Betty Hassler (LifeWay Press, 1992).

6. *I Take Thee to Be My Spouse,* compiled by David Apple (Convention Press, 1992).

7. *A Time for Healing: Coming to Terms with Your Divorce* by Harold Ivan Smith (LifeWay Press, 1994).

A N S W E R   2 4

Insuring
Marriage

Work Toward Revising State Laws to Insure Marriages

State government should not grant marriage licenses without evidence that a couple has had premarital counseling and testing to increase the odds their marriage will last.

State marital law in every state works against efforts to provide effective marriage preparation. State laws send the opposite and wrong messages to people:

• **Teen marriages are encouraged.**

Every state allows those 18 years of age and older to marry without parental consent. But many age restrictions fall well below that. With parental permission, a *girl of 12* or a *boy of 14* can marry in Massachusetts. In New Hampshire, it is 13 and 14, respectively. Most other states allow marriages at 16. Think of the strikes against the marriage when children are allowed to marry.

• **Marriages of impulse are encouraged.**

A couple that applies for a marriage license has *no waiting period* in half of the 50 United States! Most other states require only a three-day delay. The longest wait is just five days.

• **Testing is not required.**

Although most states require blood tests for

venereal disease (but not AIDS) they do not test the couple's readiness to marry and start a family.

- **No premarital counseling is required by any state.**

What sense does this make? Every state in America asks a person who wants a driver's license to pass three tests: a written test on the law; a practical, hands-on driving test; and an eye test. But no counseling or test is required to marry.

Present state law encourages quick weddings, as if deliberation in the choice of a lifelong mate were unimportant. Yet the cost of divorce to the state is immense.

Most state marriage laws remain unchanged after more than a century. In fact, *the only change has been for the worse.* Before the 1970s, a male under age 21 who wanted to marry had to have the permission of his parents. Now he can marry at 18 *without permission,* or 14 to 16 with it. How many 17-year-olds today are mature enough to choose a partner for life?

SEEK MINIMUM STATE REQUIREMENTS

Marriage should not be a light decision, made when young hormones are speaking louder than cool judgment. Rather, it should be a mature decision— agreed on by both parties and deliberated over time.

We are not realistic if we expect a state government to be as demanding as a church. However, states can require a two-month waiting period to obtain a marriage license in order to allow time for marriage preparation.

Why shouldn't states *require* a couple to present some *kind of certification* indicating they've had premarital testing, counseling, and training? The certificate could be signed by a secular counselor or by the pastor of a church.

If the state had a minimum two-month requirement for a marriage license, churches and syna-
gogues could easily require and expect four months
of marriage preparation.

State divorce laws also need to be changed. In 47
states, one person can unilaterally dissolve a marriage, even if the other person wants to reconcile.
What is worse the "innocent" party often ends up
subsidizing the person "guilty" of marital miscon-
duct.

**Consider taking on an advocacy role in seek-
ing some basic marriage law reforms for your
state.** A call to your state representative with these
concerns might open the door to effective reform in
your state.

In addition to saving marriages, states will realize
untold millions of dollars in not having to subsidize
the social ills resulting from divorce.

State governments should not grant marriages
without evidence that a couple is ready for it.

Biblical References
Psalm 106:3; 2 Corinthians 5:20; Philippians 4:8;
James 4:17

Other Resources
1. *Marriage Savers* by Michael McManus
(Zondervan, 1993), chapters 7 and 11.

A N S W E R   25

Insuring Marriage

Help Create a Community Marriage Policy

Pastors from 20 denominations in 25 cities have started reforms in many churches to radically reduce the divorce rate and been successful in saving thousands of marriages.

Being married by a pastor should have greater meaning than being married by a justice of the peace. But sadly, six in ten new marriages are failing despite the fact that 75 percent of the marriages are blessed by churches.

However, some churches truly are blessings to couples. This book has pointed to pioneering answers from the three great streams of Christianity in America: Catholic, evangelical, and mainline Protestantism.

But the churches are not learning from each other. Catholic churches require engaged couples to take a premarital inventory; meet with older, mentor couples with solid marriages; and have a minimum number of months of marriage preparation. An Episcopal church created a Marriage Ministry that saved 39 of 40 deeply troubled marriages. A United Methodist Church pioneered strategies which preserve 95 percent of stepfamilies—a contrast with the usual 60 percent divorce rate of second marriages. Southern Baptists created True Love Waits that prompted hundreds of thousands of teenagers to pledge to be chaste until they marry. Evangelicals are much more likely to ask couples living together to separate before getting married.

Therefore, when I speak to local clergy, I urge pastors of all denominations to consider creating a Community Marriage Policy that blends the best of all of these innovations. My dream is that you, your church, and your community will consider **a covenant that stretches across denominational lines—a commitment by every church in your area to demand more of engaged couples: more time, more testing, more study, and more training. And every church should offer more help to strengthen existing marriages.**

Hundreds of pastors from many denominations in two dozen diverse cities have agreed to start these reforms in a Community Marriage Policy. The result?—There were 1,210 divorces in Peoria County, IL in 1991 when clergy created the Peoria Community Marriage Policy. One year later, the number plunged to 947 divorces! And in 1993 there were only 997. Peoria has seen a one-fifth drop in the divorce rate!

Creating a Community Marriage Policy is not easy. A new resource to help is *Marriage Savers Resource Collection* which includes six videos that can make these reforms visible. Couples tell how various reforms saved their marriages. The *Collection* also includes a *Leader's Study Guide* that can be used for a 13-week adult study, *Marriage Savers*, and a copy of this book. I believe these resources can reduce the divorce rate of any church.

The *Collection* was also designed to help create a Community Marriage Policy. Here are suggestions on how to begin.

1. Ask your pastor to invite a diverse group of pastors to overview the *Collection*. Include

Catholic, mainline Protestant, evangelical, and minority pastors. Give each a copy of *Marriage Savers* and view Video 1.

2. Enlist a group of the most influential religious leaders in your community to join a Community Marriage Policy committee. If the city is large, include bishops, superintendents, or directors of mission who could prompt other pastors to become involved.

3. Encourage committee members to use *Marriage Savers Resource Collection* in their churches. This motivates them to encourage other clergy to come to a city-wide presentation of the Community Marriage Policy idea.

4. Take the initiative to mediate and negotiate the exact content of a Community Marriage Policy. There is no rigid formula. Some guidelines focus only on premarital couples. The newest policies have added guidelines encouraging chastity of teenagers and single adults. The initial task of a Community Marriage Policy committee is to thrash out their own policy.

5. Challenge the committee to enlist pastors from their denominations to attend a city-wide Community Marriage Policy adoption meeting. Experience indicates the biggest problem is getting them **to attend.** Urge as many clergy as possible to sign the policy **that day.**

6. Invite the press to attend the Community Marriage Policy adoption meeting. This is a major local story and should get good coverage. Give the press a list of all those who sign the policy. That alone will encourage many couples to work harder at their marriages, and it will encourage pastors who do not attend to join.

Sample Community Marriage Policy

Preamble

Our concern as ministers is to foster lasting marital unions under God and establish successful spiritual families. Almost 75 percent of all marriages are performed by pastors, and we are troubled by the more than 60 percent divorce rate. Our concern is to radically reduce the divorce rate among those married in area churches.

Pastors have the responsibility to raise the quality of commitment in those we marry. We believe that couples who seriously participate in premarital testing and counseling will have a better understanding of what the marriage commitment involves. As agents of God, acting on His behalf, we feel it is our responsibility to encourage couples to set aside time for marriage preparation. We acknowledge that a wedding is but a day while a marriage is for a lifetime.

We also believe that the church has an ongoing responsibility to help strengthen existing marriages and to save deeply troubled ones. "For I hate divorce, says the Lord God of Israel" (Mal. 2:16). What God has joined together, let the church help hold together.

Community Marriage Policy

1. We will encourage teenagers to sign a True Love Waits pledge and encourage older single adults to practice sexual abstinence.

2. We will offer Relationship Instruction to seriously dating couples.

3. We will require a minimum of four months marriage preparation.

4. We will require six counseling sessions, with two devoted to the use of a premarital inventory, and others on Scripture, and the substantive problems of finances, sex, communication, and conflict resolution.

5. We will train mature, married couples to serve as mentors to work with seriously dating, engaged couples, and newlyweds on a couple-to-couple basis.

6. We will encourage attendance at an Engaged Encounter weekend to help the engaged improve their communications skills, and establish their marriage with God at the center.

7. We will offer two post-marital counseling sessions with clergy or a mentor couple, six months and a year after the wedding.

8. We will encourage all married couples to attend a couple's retreat such as Marriage Encounter, Festival of Marriage, or Marriage Enrichment.

9. We will develop a Marriage Ministry of mentoring couples whose own marriage once failed to work with currently troubled marriages.

10. Those of us who are married will be the first to attend a couples' retreat.

11. We clergy will participate and cooperate fully to learn and experience more about how to help couples bond for life.

12. As clergy, we will take this policy back to our congregations to be ratified by the appropriate boards and/or congregations.

13. We will ask others to evaluate this policy.

14. We will appoint a committee of attorneys to propose changes in the state's laws of marriage and divorce.

Statement of Support

Signed:_____

Congregation:_____

Address:_____

Phone: _____

Biblical References

Deuteronomy 10:12-13; 11:18-19; Psalm 16:11; 106:35-36; Matthew 5:27-32; 1 Timothy 6:11-12

Marriage Savers Declaration

We, _____ **and** _____,
do hereby recommit our vows of marital faithfulness, in thought and deed, and promise before God that we shall stay together, from this day forward, for better or for worse; for richer or for poorer; in sickness and in health; to love, honor and cherish, until death do us part.

We also pledge our commitment to strengthen and save the marriages of others, since God hates divorce, and to establish Marriage Saver ministries in our church to help its members:

- Avoid a bad marriage before it begins;
- Give Marriage Insurance to the engaged;
- Strengthen every existing marriage;
- Save even deeply troubled marriages;
- Foster reconciliation between separated and divorced members.

Finally, we pledge to encourage our church to join with other congregations in a Community Marriage Policy to radically reduce the divorce rate where we live.

_For what God has joined together,
let the church hold together._

Agreed to by: _____
(husband)

_____
(wife)

Date: _____